$\mathcal{V}$ICTORY
without Violence

Victory without Violence

The First Ten Years of the St. Louis Committee of Racial Equality (CORE), 1947–1957

MARY KIMBROUGH AND MARGARET W. DAGEN

EDITORIAL COMMITTEE

Irvin Dagen
Margaret W. Dagen
Charles R. Oldham
Yvonne A. Rosen
Billie Teneau

University of Missouri Press • Columbia and London

Copyright © 2000 by
The Curators of the University of Missouri
University of Missouri Press, Columbia, Missouri 65201
Printed and bound in the United States of America
All rights reserved
5 4 3 2 1   04 03 02 01 00

Library of Congress Cataloging-in-Publication Data

Kimbrough, Mary.
    Victory without violence : the first ten years of the St. Louis
  Committee of Racial Equality (CORE), 1947–1957 / Mary
  Kimbrough and Margaret W. Dagen.
    p. cm.
  Includes bibliographical references and index.
  ISBN 0-8262-1303-0 (alk. paper)
    1. Afro-Americans—Segregation—Missouri—Saint Louis—
  History—20th century.   2. Afro-Americans—Civil rights—
  Missouri—Saint Louis—History—20th century.   3. St. Louis
  Committee of Racial Equality—History.   4. Civil rights move-
  ments—Missouri—Saint Louis—History—20th century.
  5. Saint Louis (Mo.)—Race relations. I. Dagen, Margaret W.,
  1919– II. Title.

F474.S29 N45 2000
323.1′196073077866—dc21   00-041795

Designer: Vickie Kersey Dubois
Typesetter: The Composing Room of Michigan, Inc.
Printer and binder: Thomson-Shore, Inc.
Typefaces: Book Antiqua, Distress, Impact, Minion

To Bernice Fisher, whose voice sounded the call to action. And to the memory of the members of the St. Louis Committee of Racial Equality who pursued a quiet but determined crusade for human rights.

In Memoriam

Jane Bowles

Clothilde Burns

Irvin Dagen

Bernice Fisher

Allyce Stewart Hamilton

Walter Hayes

Marian O'Fallon Oldham

Rose Parnas

Wanda Penny

Edgar Poindexter

Emily Cronheim Rice

Mervene Ross

Norman Winkler

Contents

ACKNOWLEDGMENTS

To those who grew up in an all-white world of segregation, the story of CORE can be an awakening. Just as clearly as we knew where the town's schools and places of worship and restaurants were located, we knew that African Americans could not enter those places, except by special permission. Most people accepted that. It was simply a way of life. The young people who organized CORE, both whites and African Americans, refused to continue that way of life. They underlined their refusal with direct, nonviolent action. What they did accept was that society had to change, and their responsibility was to help bring about that change.

That is the story recounted here, a story of long-delayed, long-opposed change, a story of courage, patience, and persistence. It is a tribute to the students, teachers, World War II veterans, and the small number of businessmen and professionals who joined together to improve the racial climate of St. Louis and to win respect for those who had long stood behind locked doors, forbidden to walk through.

To be sure, they were not alone in the battle. Others not involved with CORE, including civic activists and business leaders, clergy and laymen, students at the city's universities, and men and women of great goodwill, were concerned about opening those locked doors through other actions and in other venues. This is one chapter in the much larger story, one effort in a nationwide, midcentury crusade for human freedom. It is limited to events that took place in one crucial decade, 1947–1957.

We are deeply grateful to the members of the Editorial Committee who collected materials pertaining to the early years of CORE, searched the country for early CORE members to solicit their memories and their materials, and assisted in tape-recording interviews with early CORE members. Without their active support this account could not have been written. Billie Ames Teneau gave special attention to gathering from diverse sources copies of the CORE newsletter, *Up to Date with Core.* Charles Oldham has supported this project from its inception.

We offer our heartfelt gratitude to Bonnie Marglous Rosen for her countless hours of writing, editing, and revising, which helped us to better preserve these memories. The late Irvin Dagen researched and drafted several major sections. He guided and enriched the early efforts that he felt were important for filling a historical gap in the record of a dynamic era of change.

We are indebted to Ann Morris, Associate Director of the Western Historical Manuscript Collection at the University of Missouri–St. Louis, for helping to transfer our CORE material to the Western Historical Manuscript Collection and for technical help with research and editing. In addition, we thank Norman Seay, an early member of CORE, for his support and assistance.

We express our gratitude to Chancellor Blanche Touhill of the University of Missouri–St. Louis. As a historian, Chancellor Touhill believed that the story of CORE should be shared with future generations, and as an educator and as a citizen concerned with human rights, she was most supportive of our efforts.

VICTORY
without
Violence

From two corners of the world, from two cultures, and most of all, from the hearts of a few individuals came the inspiration for the St. Louis Committee of Racial Equality, CORE.

This is the story.

It is a story lifted from an unsung past, the story of a quiet struggle that bridged the decade between the long era of segregation and the emergence of civil rights for all men and women.

From Mahatma Gandhi came the gospel of nonviolent, active resistance to injustice and inhumanity, which became the lodestar and the mission of St. Louis CORE. From a young Chicagoan, Bernice Fisher, came information on Chicago CORE, which she, George Houser, and Jim Farmer had organized in 1942, conducting sit-ins to open public accommodations to African Americans. In 1947, Fisher inspired and motivated a small group to organize St. Louis CORE and to wage a peaceful battle in its own community against the closed-door policy that prevented nonwhites from being served at restaurants, cafeterias, lunch counters, and other public facilities. From Irv and Maggie Dagen came the initial leadership to translate ideals and hopes into action.

In 1973 August Meier and Elliott Rudwick published *CORE, A Study in the Civil Rights Movement, 1942–1968.* It offers a look at the era in which St. Louis CORE was born, an era that spawned similar local efforts across the country to counteract prejudice and discrimination. Meier and Rudwick interviewed some St. Louis CORE members about the history of their activist campaign but did not explore the origins of the local group in St. Louis. In the book they write, "This highly cohesive St. Louis chapter would prove unusually influential in CORE's history, with about half of these individuals subsequently becoming prominent in National CORE."

Bernice Fisher's local involvement began in 1947 when she came to St. Louis as an organizer for the United Wholesale and Distribution Workers of America. She was invited by the Dagens to address a meeting of Humanity, Inc., a small, diverse group of students and young adults that the Dagens had organized, which met regularly in their University City apartment. Without Fisher's challenge to the St. Louis group, it is unlikely that St. Louis CORE would have come into being that night in 1947. The story of how it all began was not reported at the time and today is almost forgotten, save by the surviving foot soldiers who served on the front lines.

It is frequently reported that the first sit-ins at lunch counters in the country took place in Greensboro, North Carolina, in 1960. The stools from the lunch counter in Greensboro where the young black demonstrators sat and waited for service are preserved at the Smithsonian Institute in Washington, D.C. But the St. Louis campaign actually preceded the one in Greensboro by almost thirteen years. Long before the demonstrators used peaceful protest in North Carolina, the members of St. Louis CORE had accepted the concept of "passive resistance" and translated that concept into "nonviolent direct action." Those revolutionary ideas took the form of interracial negotiations, sit-ins, and peaceful demonstrations.

While the absence of news coverage might appear to suggest a secretive organization, in truth St. Louis CORE was dedicated to openly communicating its aims and methods. After a long series of sit-ins at Stix, Baer & Fuller, St. Louis CORE published "A Plan for Establishing Equal Restaurant Service in St. Louis Department Stores" in

April of 1952. The plan was mailed to department store executives and civic leaders and is a good example of the polite, rational, informative manner of negotiation employed by CORE, and it gives a feeling for the atmosphere in St. Louis at that time. The plan is reproduced below in its entirety.

A Plan for Establishing Equal Restaurant Service in St. Louis Department Stores

The purpose of this plan is to focus community attention on the pattern of discrimination practiced in eating facilities by three large department stores and suggest a practical method of transposing democratic ideals to everyday living.

Color discrimination in St. Louis touches many areas of human relationships, and it is impossible to solve the problem as a whole; each area of discrimination requires different approaches and methods of change. Many groups are active in different areas, some in education, others in housing, employment, etc. Our main concern has been with eating facilities in the downtown and midtown areas. The department stores welcome Negro patronage in most parts of their stores, but exclude Negroes from nearly all their eating facilities. It seems logical to us that these stores should be among the first to change their policies.

We realize that this plan is far from perfect and welcome constructive criticism from interested groups or individuals. It is a plan, however, which permits flexibility and provides a method of positive, gradual change.

Some eight years ago, department store representatives met with community leaders and the Mayor's Race Relations Council, discussed the inadequacy of eating facilities for Negroes in the downtown area, and agreed that some action must be taken. Shortly thereafter, the department stores opened limited facilities to Negroes: these were the basement cafeteria at Scruggs, Vandervoort, Barney, a basement lunch counter in Stix, Baer and Fuller, and a basement balcony lunch counter at Famous-Barr. Recent talks with department store officials indicate that the operation of these integrated eating facilities has been highly successful.

About four years ago CORE (Committee of Racial Equality) approached the department stores and asked that everyone be given service in all the stores' eating facilities. The request was met with a great deal of opposition, the stores contending that other areas in the city had not progressed as far as they. After several months of negotiations and public-protest demonstrations, it was apparent that the department stores would not consider a policy change at that time. The department store problem was discussed at several CORE meetings, and it was decided that other stores in the downtown area should also be approached. CORE then directed its attention to dime stores, drug stores and certain other facilities. CORE's approach has been singularly successful and many of the places listed on the last page of this plan adopted democratic policies only after being approached by CORE.

The community pattern of St. Louis is a changing one. It is moving from a racially segregated to an integrated society. Many areas of the city are integrated and other areas are in the process of change. Practically all city facilities are open to everyone. This includes parks and recreation facilities, Kiel Auditorium, the Municipal Athletic League, the Municipal Opera and public libraries. Public transportation operates on a non-segregated basis. Many schools have changed their policies—the Catholic Schools, St. Louis University, and the graduate and professional schools of Washington University. Racial barriers are crumbling in local movie theaters: the Shady Oak, Aubert, Uptown, Art, Lynn, and all drive-in theaters admit everyone. For the past several years, there has been no racial segregation at Sportsman's Park, the Arena or at Walsh Stadium. Progress is also being made in other areas such as hotels and employment.

Besides those eating facilities in which a policy change has already been made, there are seven stores in the downtown and midtown area that are currently conducting CORE-arranged experiments in integrated eating, with a view toward a complete opening of their facilities. At these stores Negro and interracial groups of two or three people eat at specified times with management approval as a means of preparing both store employees and customers for the complete change. This plan provides a means for making a gradual but complete policy change with a minimum of tension. The experiences at these stores have been very gratifying; management and testing groups have not encountered any unpleasant repercussions.

Recently, CORE asked the department stores to allow experimental testing to take place in their eating facilities. Officials of the stores, however, have said that they cannot make a policy change or allow tests to be conducted in their stores because their customers will object. We believe they are mistaken. We believe that many groups and individuals want a policy change and would endorse a plan setting forth a positive and realistic approach to the problem. Accordingly, CORE proposes the following step by step method of opening the department store facilities:

First—A meeting of the three department store managers with representatives of interested groups to agree on a gradual opening of the stores' eating facilities.

Second—The setting up of a time table of prearranged eating tests by small interracial groups at various eating facilities of the stores.

Third—At the end of the agreed testing period, another conference would be held, the experiences

of the test groups evaluated and more tests planned
or a complete opening agreed upon.

Fourth—No newspaper publicity about the tests
should be given during the execution of this plan.

In addition to the limited department store facilities, these eating places serve everyone:

CHIPPEWA DRUG STORE
Grand and Washington

CHIPPEWA DRUG STORE
Grand and St. Louis

SEARS, ROEBUCK AND CO.
1408 N. Kingshighway

SEARS, ROEBUCK AND CO.
3708 S. Grand

WALGREEN'S DRUG STORE
6693 Delmar

WALGREEN'S DRUG STORE
4977 Delmar

WALGREEN'S DRUG STORE
6116 Easton

WALGREEN'S DRUG STORE
500 N. Grand

WALGREEN'S DRUG STORE
3101 S. Grand

WALGREEN'S DRUG STORE
4 Hampton Village Plaza

WALGREEN'S DRUG STORE
811 Washington

WALGREEN'S DRUG STORE
7374 Manchester

WALGREEN'S DRUG STORE
1000 Olive

GREYHOUND BUS TERMINAL
701 N. Broadway

EAST ST. LOUIS BUS TERMINAL
4th and Washington

DOWNTOWN YMCA
1528 Locust

DOWNTOWN YWCA
1411 Locust

MUNICIPAL ART MUSEUM
Forest Park

FRED HARVEY RESTAURANT
18th and Market

SCHNEITHORST'S RESTAURANT
Lambert Field Airport

By April 1952, five years after CORE began, the eating establishments listed above were open to all as a result of
CORE's efforts.

Despite CORE's visibility, the major St. Louis daily
newspapers paid little or no notice to their protests.
Richard Dudman, retired chief Washington correspondent for the *St. Louis Post-Dispatch,* recalled in a commentary on the Op-Ed page of the June 11, 1990, *St. Louis Post-
Dispatch* how as a young reporter in the mid–1940s he
wanted to report on a sit-in at a major St. Louis department store, but he was told by an editor that "the newspaper knows all about it, and there is no need for a story."
Dudman called two retired editors, who confirmed his
recollection. He wrote:

> [They] still generally maintain that the policy was
> appropriate, considering racial tension at the time,
> earlier interracial violence in St. Louis and the in-
> fluence of such racists as Gerald L. K. Smith in the

COMMENTARY

St. Louis' Silent Racial Revolution

Newspapers Did Not Cover Campaign To Integrate Lunch Counters

By Richard Dudman

Historians have thus far neglected to give the Midwest, and St. Louis in particular, its rightful credit for its role in an early phase of the civil rights movement. Most histories date the lunch-counter sit-ins from Feb. 1, 1960, when four black college students sat, unserved, at the counter of the Woolworth store in Greensboro, N.C., until the store closed for the day.

The campaign continued, drawing local and national press coverage and spreading quickly to other cities. The sit-ins, which included white students, showed the unstoppable power of nonviolent protest and became the forerunners of the freedom rides, marches and boycotts that led to the end of Jim Crow and the eventual victory of the civil rights movement. Actually, the sit-ins started considerably earlier than 1960. I remember happening upon a sit-in at a downtown St. Louis lunch counter in about 1950, shortly after I joined the *Post-Dispatch* as a reporter. Blacks and whites were occupying all the stools. No one was being served. I asked what was going on and was told it was a demonstration by the Committee of Racial Equality (CORE). As I recall, an editor told me the newspaper knew all about it and there was no need for a story. A recent check of the *Post-Dispatch* files turned up no stories about those lunch counter sit-ins.

Among present-day St. Louisans who took part in those early sit-ins are Norman Seay and Charles Oldham. Both say the campaign went on for many months in the late 1940s or early 1950s and that they understood at the time that the *Post-Dispatch, Globe-Democrat* and *Star-Times* all had a policy against publishing news of the sit-ins.

Irvin Dagen, now a St. Louis attorney, and his wife, Margaret, were among the founders of CORE in St. Louis. They say they heard about "nonviolent direct action" from Bernice Fisher, a former theology student in Chicago who had become a labor union organizer and was brought to St. Louis by Harold Gibbons of the Teamsters' Union. She told them that such methods had been used successfully in Chicago and Detroit.

The Dagens knew that many blacks avoided going downtown at midday because the only place they could eat lunch were some small restaurants where customers stood at the counter. It was the era of the "vertical Negro," in Harry Golden's phrase. This form of segregation was a matter of custom, not law, but it was nonetheless rigid.

A black woman sometimes would take a sandwich in her purse and eat her lunch in the lavatory in one of the department stores.

According to the Dagens, a mixed group of three or four dozen people, about evenly divided between blacks and whites, planned the campaign to desegregate St. Louis lunch counters. They kept no secrets. They told the police and their friends at the newspapers what they planned to do. And before tackling a business, they always asked to see the manager, tried to negotiate an end to discrimination and, if that failed, disclosed their plan of action.

A downtown Katz Drug Store was their first target. As Margaret Dagen remembers it, no sit-in was necessary there. The management permitted two blacks to come in and be served each day for several weeks to get the counter personnel and other customers used to the idea of an integrated lunch counter, later opening the counter to anyone.

When it was clear that there was going to be no trouble over desegregation at the St. Louis store, the committee met with Katz executives in Kansas City and negotiated integration of Katz lunch counters throughout the region.

In other cases, prolonged sit-ins proved to be the only way to persuade managements to negotiate a settlement. The sit-in at Stix, Baer & Fuller went on for more than a year, says Dagen.

Eventually, all of the major lunch counters were desegregated, including those at Stix, and at Scruggs, Vandervoort & Barney, Famous-Barr, Walgreens and Woolworth's — all without serious incident.

In some cases, she says, a business firm would ask CORE, as part of a negotiated settlement, to join in preventing any publicity. Some businesses that agreed to desegregate their lunch counters early in the campaign expressed fear that news stories about the move would cause a sudden rush of blacks, lined up for blocks to take advantage of the new policy.

Actually, it took the black community some time to get used to open lunch counters, and black customers arrived only gradually, recalls Margaret Dagen. She says, however, that the group always agreed, when asked, to do its best to prevent publicity. But she adds that the newspapers had shown so little interest in the campaign that there never was much chance that a news story would appear.

Two retired *Post-Dispatch* editors who were not then in policy-making positions confirm the paper's policy of not publishing news of the lunch counter sit-ins. The two, Selwyn Pepper and Evarts A. Graham, still generally maintain that the policy was appropriate, considering racial tension at the time, earlier interracial violence in St. Louis and the influence of such racists as Gerald L.K. Smith in the community. They say publicizing the sit-ins might have triggered renewed violence, and they credit the news blackout in part for the fact that lunch-counter integration proceeded peacefully in St. Louis.

In hindsight, Graham says the *Post-Dispatch* perhaps should have published an explanatory article about the movement and its strategy, without naming the particular sites of the sit-ins.

One result of the news blackout is that the history books do not yet mention an innovative, peaceful and successful St. Louis venture in breaking down racial segregation. Another result seems to have been that most of the country had to wait nearly a decade before the lunchrooms began to abandon Jim Crow.

Richard Dudman, Ellsworth, Maine, was a reporter for the Post-Dispatch *for 31 years until he retired in 1981 as chief Washington correspondent.*

community. They say publicizing the sit-ins might
have triggered renewed violence, and they credit
the news blackout in part for the fact that lunch-
counter integration proceeded peacefully in St.
Louis. . . . One result of the news blackout is that
the history books do not yet mention an innovative,
peaceful and successful St. Louis venture in breaking down racial segregation.

CORE members did not seek publicity. However, they
believe that today, a half century later, their story is well
worth the telling, so that a generation accustomed to open
public accommodations will know and understand what
has gone before. This is the story of a decade, a minuscule
niche in human history, in which a small crusade brought
about a change in public perceptions and attitudes and,
finally, in policy. During World War II, segregated black
troops had fought with the same valor as white troops.
When that war was over, life seemed peaceful and good.
Few realized how strong the winds of change were blowing. It was a time of transition, when blacks sensed a new
potential for freedom. It was a time when some blacks and
whites, concerned with social injustice, sought means
to turn that potential into reality, while others remained
opposed, indifferent, or unaware.

This, then, is an effort to reconstruct, for history's sake,
a pivotal series of events in St. Louis: the end of injustice
in one aspect of race relations. This history is told with admiration for the partners, black and white, who joined in
the adventure to right a wrong in the human experience.
It is compiled from the memories of those partners and
from the early records of the St. Louis chapter of CORE.
"We wish now we had retained all minutes, leaflets, correspondence with store owners and managers and other
records," said one of the early members, "but at the time

we were not self-conscious about making history, just in making change in race relations."

In 1994, a small group of early CORE members set out to rectify that oversight. They called on as many of their former colleagues as they could trace to create a "collection of our memories that will be useful for continuing our struggle to achieve a cohesive, multicultural society in which people can live in good spirit and peace with each other." Many of the quotations that appear throughout this account are from responses they received.

Bernice Fisher was the catalyst for that struggle. Many shared her dream and her vision. But some, like her, did not live to see the closed doors swing open.

One

A Nation of Closed Doors

The time was right. Although few recognized the signs, America—and St. Louis—were ready for a new concept of social justice. World War II was over, and in its wake old traditions were dying. In scattered places throughout the country, men and women who opposed society's deep-seated racism were igniting the fires of what would become a social revolution. In an apartment in University City, then an all-white community where African Americans were not welcome, a small group became a part of that nascent movement. Dedicated to the nonviolent philosophy of Mahatma Gandhi, they set out peacefully, with determination and dignity, to make a difference. This is their story, the story of CORE.

The year was 1947. Two years earlier World War II had ended in a euphoria of peace; now a struggle on the home front had to be waged.

Even before the war, Americans had been forced to think about human suffering and how to alleviate it. When the stock market had crashed and the gaudy 1920s had given way to the grim 1930s, the good times had disappeared. In their place had come the Great Depression, the New Deal, the WPA, the PWA, the CCC, and the dreary trek of the poor from the Dust Bowl in search of employment. In the 1940s, the world went through a cataclysmic war. In its aftermath, the disruption in family and community life and the overturning of the status quo were continuing to ferment in bitter counterpoint to the joy of victory.

American society would never be the same, and that was good as well as bad. One of the salutary effects of social turmoil was the change taking place in the hearts and minds of people everywhere. During the Great Depression, the critical needs had been food and shelter and jobs. In wartime, the nation closed ranks, made sacrifices at home, and worked for victory abroad. At midcentury, with the good times returning, America could not continue the earlier pattern of discrimination that had closed many doors to African Americans in the workplace, in schools, in housing, in hotels, in sports, in eating places, in theaters, and even in most churches.

Some Americans were developing an awareness of human injustice and a hunger for healing. Early evidence of that awareness and hunger was the announcement in 1941 that A. Philip Randolph was prepared to organize a peaceful March on Washington (MOW) to protest the exclusion of blacks from the defense industries. Randolph was the national president of the Brotherhood of Sleeping Car Porters. An impressive and influential leader, he was known as "the Gandhi of the Negroes," because of his adherence to passive, nonviolent resistance.

James Farmer, one of the founders of Chicago CORE, wrote in his autobiography, *Lay Bare the Heart,* that Randolph "roared through the country holding 'monster mass meetings,' telling the crowds about the outrage of booming war industries in America, the arsenal of the fight for freedom, which still discriminated against blacks. Roosevelt . . . was terrified that the march would embarrass him in the world community at a time when he was trying to put a great and clean face forward."

Bargaining with Randolph, Roosevelt agreed that if the march were called off, he would issue an executive order outlawing racial discrimination in the defense industries and establishing a Fair Employment Practices Commission to investigate instances of such discrimination. Roosevelt issued Executive Order 8802, requiring fair employment practices in the federal government, and Randolph called off the march. Even with the executive order, actual changes were slow, and the level of jobs offered to African Americans varied greatly.

Randolph remained a towering leader in the civil rights movement. He and Theodore McNeal, St. Louis field representative for the Brotherhood of Sleeping Car Porters and later Missouri's first black state senator, often visited the apartment of Irv and Maggie Dagen, brought there by Bernice Fisher in her early days in St. Louis. Maggie recalled, "We had some wonderful discussions and learned and learned and learned."

Fisher told the Dagens about her involvement with CORE, the Committee of Racial Equality, in Chicago. She told about meeting George Houser and Jim Farmer while she was a graduate student studying theology at the University of Chicago. Houser and Farmer were pacifists working for the Fellowship of Reconciliation (FOR). FOR was an integrated organization of Christian pacifists that rejected violence and war and counseled conscientious objectors. Fisher told how Jim Farmer had developed a plan for a nationwide interracial Gandhian movement to end segregation. He proposed using nonviolent direct action, including noncooperation and civil disobedience. Fisher said that in April 1942, she and Farmer and Houser and other students, including Jim Robinson, an English major at the University of Chicago and a member of several pacifist groups; Homer Jack, a student at Meadville School of Theology and a member of FOR; Joe Guinn, a youth coordinator for the Chicago NAACP; Bob Chino, a half-Chinese, half-Caucasian student at the University of

Chicago; and Hugo Victoreen, had organized CORE. Chino had come up with the name. Originally CORE had been a subsidiary of FOR, limited to operating in Chicago and restricted from competing with FOR for funds or memberships on a national level. Fisher told how Chicago CORE had organized the first orderly, friendly sit-in at the Jack Spratt Coffee House in the spring of 1942. She also recounted CORE's efforts to integrate the White City Roller Skating Rink in Chicago that spring, and she described Boy's Fellowship House, an interracial living cooperative in a large house in the until-then all-white Hyde Park neighborhood of Chicago. The Dagens were enthusiastic about all she described. But Maggie said, "We are several hundred miles south of Chicago. Do you think it can work here?" And Bernice Fisher urged them to try.

Civil rights became a litmus test for liberals and a Sword of Damocles in political campaigns of the 1940s. In the Democratic party, with its historic southern base, conservatives determined to maintain segregation at all costs split from their northern and moderate Midwestern colleagues to form the Dixiecrats.

In 1944, the Supreme Court outlawed all-white primaries, increasing the number of black voters and thus strengthening the voice of blacks. African Americans gained representation in state legislatures in both the north and south and in the United States Congress. This led to the questioning of Jim Crow in daily life and in the politics of the south. In 1948, President Truman delivered the first civil rights message to Congress, ordered the integration of the armed services, and issued an executive order banning discrimination in the hiring of federal employees. In the election that year, Democrat Truman's victory stunned a confident Republican Thomas E. Dewey, and the subject of racial inequality became a highly visible issue.

National and local organizations pushed for desegregation, and there were successes. The courts became more actively involved. Thurgood Marshall, attorney for the NAACP and later the first African American on the U.S. Supreme Court, came to St. Louis to gather information for court cases on discrimination. *Negroes: Their Gift to St. Louis,* a book published by the Employee Loan Company, notes in its section on human rights:

> The St. Louis branch of The National Association for the Advancement of Colored People, one of the largest and most active in the nation, has advanced many successful educational and legal projects in voter registration, public accommodations, public school education, labor relations, apprenticeship training, housing and employment. The branch played a major role in having the David Ranken, Jr., School of Mechanical Trades open its doors to Negroes. . . .
>
> Two of the branch's legal cases drew national attention and won favorable decisions by the United States Supreme Court. One, the famous landmark case, *Missouri ex rel Gaines v. Canada,* in 1938, opened graduate training in law to Negroes in Missouri. The other, *Shelley v. Kraemer,* in 1948, overturned restrictive covenants in housing.
>
> The case of *Davis v. The St. Louis Housing Authority* resulted in the opening of all low rent public housing on a non-segregated basis. St. Louis attorneys Henry D. Espy and Sidney R. Redmond, aided by famed NAACP lawyer, Charles Houston, helped to win the Gaines case while attorney George L. Vaughn did the same for the restrictive housing case. Attorneys Frankie Freeman and Robert L. Witherspoon gave legal leadership to the public housing suit.

Frankie Freeman became associate general counsel for the St. Louis Housing Authority, and President Lyndon

Johnson later appointed her to the Federal Civil Rights Commission.

Commenting on the Shelley and Gaines decisions, Irv Dagen, founder of St. Louis CORE, said:

> The Supreme Court ruled that racially restrictive covenants were unenforceable; not that the covenants in themselves were invalid, but that attempted enforcement was unconstitutional, considered as state action in violation of the 14th Amendment. An anomaly in the Gaines case was that it established the right of Negroes to legal education within the state of Missouri, but the law school established in St. Louis was both segregated and very inadequate.

These court actions showed a growing opposition to the status quo that was reflected by Truman's election in 1948. They were the prelude to a new view of the civil rights movement that would fully emerge in the 1950s and 1960s.

In his Civil Rights Address of 1948, President Truman called for a permanent Fair Employment Practices Commission, but passage was blocked by southern Democrats. When Truman addressed the 1948 Jackson Day Dinner, the table reserved for southern Democrats was empty. Still, Hubert Humphrey was able to include a liberal civil rights plank in the 1948 party platform.

During the 1940s, social activists, aware of increasing discontent with the status quo, promoted social, judicial, and legislative change. Following the 1946 U.S. Supreme Court decision revoking Jim Crow laws in interstate travel, FOR organized the first freedom ride into the south to challenge Jim Crow practices. George Houser told the freedom ride story in his book, *No One Can Stop the Rain:*

> Bayard Rustin and I collaborated with others on a song that we would sing at public gatherings to the

tune of the spiritual "No Hidin' Place Down Here."
The first verse went:

> You don't have to ride Jim Crow,
> You don't have to ride Jim Crow.
> On June the 3rd,
> The High Court said
> When you ride interstate
> Jim Crow is dead,
> You don't have to ride Jim Crow.

Men returning from military service formed the American Veterans Committee, in Washington, D.C., with the stated objective of "achieving a more democratic and prosperous America and a more stable world." They championed civil rights, but resistance to civil rights endured. Even though African Americans had faced the same dangers and fought as valiantly as whites in World War II, they had not attained equality on the home front where segregation and prejudice remained strong, and doors remained closed.

It is in this turbulent, inhospitable climate that the story of the St. Louis Committee of Racial Equality begins.

Two

A Crack in the Door

The St. Louis Committee of Racial Equality had few members, but it was spirited and staunch. It was destined to play a vital role in the battle for human justice; however, CORE did not stand alone. Its image must be superimposed on the larger portrait of a community and of a nation, a portrait reflecting struggle, turmoil, and a new vision of social action. Produced by a confluence of new thought and activity that, even in 1947, was creating a social revolution throughout America, CORE helped change the racial climate in St. Louis and facilitated acceptance of that change.

Many of the early members of the St. Louis chapter of CORE were students at Washington University, a segregated private university in St. Louis. Student veterans had tried, without success, to change the university's admissions policy. When the Washington University American Veterans Committee dissolved in 1947, its leaders joined students from the campus YMCA and YWCA and the George Warren Brown School of Social Work to form the Student Committee for the Admission of Negroes (SCAN). They led a determined and courageous campaign to open classroom doors to all, despite the unwillingness of the administration and trustees.

In the winter 1989–1990 issue of *Gateway Heritage,* published by the Missouri Historical Society, Amy M. Pfeiffenberger explored the Washington University situation in depth, particularly the role of SCAN's campaign for admission of African Americans. She reported that in 1946

Washington University "was finding it increasingly difficult to ignore mounting public sentiment and maintain its
segregationist policy. . . . Civil rights activists, students
and individuals from the community had awakened to
the contradiction implicit in fighting what was in part a
war against racism abroad while upholding segregation
at home."

Particularly vocal were the students themselves, most
of whom were reported to be either actively or passively
supporting the admission of African Americans. At the in-
sistence of Dean Benjamin Youngdahl, the school of social
work desegregated in 1948. Some of the other graduate
programs followed suit, but the liberal arts college and
other divisions of the university remained an all-white
world. A SCAN-sponsored student poll in 1949 resulted
in a 77.4 percent favorable vote for the admission of
blacks. Despite peaceful picketing and continued pressure on the administration, officials merely acknowl-
edged student demands and refused to change school policy. The faculty was divided or indifferent on the issue.

But the pressure finally proved effective. On Friday,
May 9, 1952, the administration and trustees of Washington University quietly passed a resolution to open the
doors, desegregating the undergraduate divisions. It was
eight years after Patrick J. Holleran S.J., president of Saint
Louis University, had announced that his school would
admit African Americans, making the Jesuit university
the first school in the state to integrate.

As the Washington University students were protesting
the closed-door policy, Irv and Maggie Dagen, long committed to the cause of minority and racial equality, welcomed them and others of like mind to their University
City apartment for regular discussions of social issues.
They named their group Humanity, Inc. Out of it would

come the St. Louis chapter of CORE. For the meetings Maggie, who was teaching senior courses in labor relations and human relations at Clayton High School, borrowed folding chairs from a local funeral home, and Irv, a partner in a leather-importing firm, invited labor leaders, political leaders, lawyers, reporters, and professors to speak. Local, state, and national labor leaders, Canadian Labor Party leader David Lewis, former Warsaw City Council member Dr. Jerzy Gliksman, the British Consul assigned to St. Louis, reporters from the *St. Louis Post-Dispatch*, the president of the St. Louis Chapter of the NAACP, and many professors and students led discussions on such topics as the Taft-Hartly Act, the success of the Marshall Plan, Henry Wallace and the Progressive Citizens of America, community pressure to integrate Washington University, Soviet policy in world affairs, the merger of the A F of L and the CIO, Communist infiltration of unions, the U.S. occupation forces in Korea, Great Britain's nationalization of industry, the philosophy of Mahatma Gandhi, treason in the era of Joe McCarthy, and the race question.

"We were seeking something we lacked on campus, a forum for intelligent consideration of social, economic and political problems of our time," said Bonnie Marglous Rosen, an early member. "Irv was willing to provide it for us. In fact, he became our honorary professor, guide, and mentor in the university of life." Her sister, Doris Marglous Nugent, recalled, "We both went to meetings at the Dagens' in the Delmar Loop where politics, philosophy and the realities behind international affairs were discussed and argued with passion. It was out of this concern for social justice that CORE was born."

Invited to speak at one of the meetings of Humanity, Inc., in 1947, Bernice Fisher galvanized the group into action that was destined to alter the racial climate of St. Louis. In 1947, Fisher was living in St. Louis, working as an organizer for the United Wholesale and Distribution Workers of America, which would later become a strong local of the Teamsters Union. In his autobiography, *Lay Bare the Heart*, James Farmer described Fisher as combining a

> fiery hatred of racism with a violent rejection of war. Both evils made her fighting mad. I often called her the most warlike pacifist I ever knew. The bombs that fell on Pearl Harbor caused the intensity of her feelings toward race and war to become even more explosive. . . . She prided herself in color blindness. . . . Bernice was a passionately committed religious pacifist and a Norman Thomas socialist.

Farmer went on to say that Fisher "was intrigued to learn that I was preparing for a Gandhi-type of non-violent direct action against segregation and race discrimination." When she heard of Farmer's plan, Fisher exclaimed, "Thank God! At last, maybe we can turn this nation around. It's the most exciting idea I've ever heard!"

"That was the Bernice Fisher who inspired us, in 1947, in St. Louis, to organize the local CORE group," said Irv Dagen. "From her, via CORE, came a more open St. Louis community. That's why this writing [*Victory without Violence*] is dedicated to her with thanks and appreciation."

Bernice Fisher brought the message and the experience of Chicago CORE to the St. Louis group in 1947. Thus, out of this diverse discussion group emerged the solid center of St. Louis CORE. Fisher's listeners that night in the University City apartment did not want merely to talk and theorize about prejudice and discrimination. They were primed for action. After Fisher had described Chicago

CORE's sit-ins, she was asked if the same kind of protest could be tried in St. Louis.

"Why not?" she replied.

And so it was decided. A number of those who attended Humanity, Inc., determined to do something. They formed a group called the Committee of Racial Equality, or St. Louis CORE. It was inspired by Chicago CORE and helped create a national presence for the organization, but it was autonomous and had no formal ties to the older group. St. Louis CORE would work to open the doors of various public accommodations, particularly eating establishments, to everyone, starting in thriving downtown St. Louis.

With its decision to target public accommodations, CORE carved out its own niche. With its philosophy of direct action and nonviolence, CORE found a way to first open the door a crack and then widen the crack. The early members could have chosen another problem, but they were pragmatic idealists. Other organizations in the field of race relations, such as the Urban League and the NAACP, focused on discrimination in employment, housing, neighborhood improvements, and educational opportunities. The closed-door policy adopted by many St. Louis eating establishments was a manageable problem, serious enough to be tackled but narrow enough for their numbers and resources to handle.

If, in their youth and their passion for justice, early CORE members had thought about the road ahead, they might have been discouraged. They should have known they would encounter bumps and potholes. As Irv Dagen pointed out, this was, after all, St. Louis, Missouri:

> St. Louis, in the pre–Civil War days and in the Civil War, was neither all north nor south, containing abolitionists and slave holders, Blues and Grays, segre-

gationists and those who were opposed. This left
many areas open to discrimination, to custom and
tradition, and left open the possibility for peaceful
change on which CORE could capitalize.

Although early CORE did not have a specific date of organization, charter members, or annual dues, it did have
rules of conduct to implement its philosophy. Its membership changed through the years as some people became less active and others took their places. The earliest
participants in St. Louis CORE were young idealists. They
were an integrated group of students, graduates, and faculty from Washington University, Stowe Teachers College, Saint Louis University, and a few local high schools.
There were veterans, teachers, lawyers, postal workers, a
labor organizer, and social workers. Many became interested in the philosophy of Mahatma Gandhi, who was
constantly in the news as he used nonviolent, passive resistance to bring about the independence of India from
Great Britain and a change in social conditions on the
other side of the globe.

Irv Dagen had grown up in Brooklyn, New York, influ-
enced by the liberal political and social ideas that he
heard vigorously debated at home, at Columbia University, and as a writer for the WPA Writers' Project in New
York. He came to St. Louis in 1940 as a partner in a
leather-importing firm, and his business often took him
to Mexico, Haiti, and Guatemala. While working as an
importer, he attended Saint Louis University's law school
at night, and in 1954, at age forty-one, he began practicing law. Through his new career, he continued his quest
for social justice.

Maggie Dagen's philosophy was shaped by her mother's Quaker background and by her father's deep respect
for people of different nationalities. His respect resulted

from his career as chief attorney for the U.S. Immigration and Naturalization Service in St. Louis, a position he held from 1914 until his retirement in 1950. Maggie received a master's degree from Northwestern University, worked in war plants, and then pursued a Ph.D. in labor relations at Cornell University. In 1945 she returned home to St. Louis to continue her degree work at Washington University while teaching social studies at Clayton High School.

One day, while shopping in downtown St. Louis, she experienced a disturbing incident. She encountered an African American woman who was eating a sandwich in a small, dim rest room of a major department store. She asked her why she was eating there. "Because I'm not permitted to sit at the lunch counter," was the answer. Maggie realized that the scene was being repeated over and over throughout the city as victims of discrimination sought to cope with life in a segregated world. "Blacks did not live in a land where all people had elbow room and freedom to go into a restaurant, a movie, a hotel, a bowling alley," recalled Maggie. "When they wanted to shop downtown, as they had every right to do, they either planned their shopping to avoid meals or they would put a sandwich in their pocket or purse and go into a rest room to eat it, and that offended me."

Charles Oldham was a veteran from the Army Air Force and a student at the Washington University School of Law, where he was a charter member of the American Veterans Committee and a strong supporter of the admission of African Americans. Oldham graduated and began practicing law in 1947, but while he was still a student he was invited by Maggie Dagen, one of his instructors at Washington University, to attend the meetings of Humanity, Inc. In 1997 he wrote to the Dagens:

> I now understand the metamorphosis that resulted
> from those meetings at your home. It was at this time
> that I began to see dimly that all was not as I had
> been taught. Fortunately the lessons and informa-
> tion fell on somewhat fertile ground and it started
> me toward a different and more rewarding life. . . .
> There were a lot of us whose lives were changed for
> the better by those thought sessions.

Marian O'Fallon had graduated from Stowe Teachers
College, the black teachers' college run by the St. Louis
Public Schools. She was teaching kindergarten in one of
the black elementary schools in St. Louis. She typed some
of the legal briefs for *Shelley v. Kraemer,* the case about re-
strictive covenants that went to the Supreme Court, and
she picketed at the American Theater before she became
involved in CORE. She later married Charles Oldham and
became a well-known educator and community leader.

Margie Toliver and Jane Bowles were both students at
Stowe Teachers College. Joe Ames, a student at the Washington University School of Law, was a World War II veteran who had been awarded a Purple Heart. He was active with the American Veterans Committee and SCAN
and later became an organizer for the Teamsters Union.
His wife, Billie, was a housewife with two young children,
a typewriter, and a telephone that she put to good use on
behalf of CORE.

Marvin Rich was a Washington University student and
a SCAN activist. He attended the forums at the Dagens'
apartment, helped found St. Louis CORE, and after a stint
in the army during the Korean War, became the staff person in charge of community relations for national CORE.

The Marglous sisters, Bonnie and Doris, were Ethical
Society members and graduates of University City High
School. As Washington University students they had

protested with SCAN. They participated in Humanity, Inc. from its inception. Bonnie went on to the George Warren Brown School of Social Work at Washington University. Mary McClain was the fourth African American student to enroll in the George Warren Brown School of Social Work before Washington University opened its undergraduate divisions to blacks. McClain was from Pueblo, Colorado, and had not experienced segregation until she came to St. Louis.

Rose and Jerry Parnas were Washington University students active in SCAN. Rose was especially sensitive to discrimination because of painful early experiences as the only Jewish child in her elementary school.

After serving in the army in World War II, Steve Best came to St. Louis to join Cecil Hinshaw's Peace Army, a small group that visited churches to spread the doctrine of Gandhi. He stayed to work at the Missouri Welfare Department, and there he met his future wife, Joyce. Steve was attracted to CORE because of its emphasis on the nonviolent, passive resistance advocated by Gandhi.

Irene Williams was an African American student in speech and language therapy at St. Louis University when she helped CORE to integrate eating establishments near the university. Vivian Dreer, a daughter of the highly respected African American educator Herman Dreer, grew up in the segregated city of St. Louis and was teaching at Vashon High School. She became acquainted with Marian O'Fallon, who was typing Herman Dreer's Ph.D. dissertation on "Negro Leadership in St. Louis, A Study in Race Relations," and Marian persuaded Vivian to get involved in CORE.

Walter Hayes was a postal employee and a World War II veteran who was frustrated at having fought in a segregated Marine Corps. He learned of CORE while playing bridge at an integrated community center. For a while Walter shared an apartment in north St. Louis with Charles Oldham. Wanda Penny was a beautiful, stately, artistic woman who became involved in CORE while she was a student at Stowe Teachers College.

Henry Hodge grew up in the black ghetto in St. Louis and became active in the Young People's Group at the Ethical Society. There he met Joe Ames, who invited him to participate in CORE. Edgar Poindexter was a postal employee and a friend of Walter Hayes's and Marian O'Fallon's.

Al Park, a veteran of World War II and an employee of Bemis Bag Company, was a friend of Irv and Maggie Dagen's. Al and his wife, Ann, joined CORE in 1949. Norman Winkler, another veteran of World War II, had been twice awarded the Bronze Star for heroism. At Washington University he was active in the American Veterans Committee and SCAN.

Clothilde Burns was one of the early African American graduate students at Washington University when she began attending CORE meetings and sitting-in at Stix, Baer & Fuller; Scruggs, Vandervoort, Barney; and an ice cream shop at the corner of Page and Walton. Norman Seay, a student at Vashon High School in St. Louis, was active in an organization called Intergroup Youth; he met Maggie Dagen at a meeting of that organization, an integrated group of students and teachers.

Also among the early members of CORE were two Washington University professors: Arnold Rose, an eminent sociologist, and Huston Smith, a professor of comparative religion. Rose had assisted Gunnar Myrdal, the Swedish sociologist, in the preparation of his influential book on race, *An American Dilemma.* Smith had authored *The Religions of Man,* a guide that continues to be a popular authority on the world's religions. Their wives, Caroline Rose and Eleanor Smith, also were early CORE participants.

They were a disparate group—black and white, professionals and students. They came from many backgrounds and were attracted to CORE for different reasons. But they bonded in the common hope of creating a more just community. The need for their work was underscored by the fact that Seay's mother feared for her son's safety when he took the streetcar and then walked through an all-white neighborhood to the Dagens' University City apartment. Walter Hayes, who found his way to CORE in 1948, spoke for many black veterans when he wrote of his CORE experience:

> I suppose I became a dedicated member of CORE because I was looking for ways to channel my anger, frustration and resentment at having grown up and lived in a segregated society in both Arkansas and Missouri, and experiencing four years of the same segregation in the Marine Corps in World War II, from 1942 to 1946. After fighting in a war for the United States and coming out alive, I was determined not to take any more second-hand treatment and had already, on my own, stopped accepting any form of segregation. I think many military blacks had the same mind-set.

Downtown eating establishments had long closed their doors to blacks. In the downtown area an African American could not sit at a counter or a table and order a meal. In the downtown dime stores, only stand-up counters would serve blacks, and few of them provided good service, a pleasant atmosphere, or an open welcome.

The one exception was a basement cafeteria at Scruggs, Vandervoort, Barney, a major department store. Scruggs had opened its cafeteria in 1944 as a result of sit-ins by the Citizens Civil Rights Commission, a group of black and white women led by Pearl Maddox, a widow; Henry Wheeler, a postal worker; David Grant, an attorney; and Theodore McNeal, a field representative for the Brotherhood of Sleeping Car Porters.

In Missouri, eating establishments were segregated by custom, not by law. Only school integration and interracial marriage were prohibited by Missouri's constitution. Yet, custom had become as strong a deterrent as the constitution, a city ordinance, or a police officer's badge. Most residents of St. Louis and of America just shrugged their shoulders, if they noticed at all. Yet by the end of the twentieth century, most whites would be able to recall only faintly the discrimination of the past. Even though those over fifty grew up with it, they lived with it without really seeing it. However, a few people had recognized the evil of discrimination, and it gnawed at their consciences. And so, in this soil of prejudice, CORE took root in the collective conscience of a diverse, integrated group.

Some of its members were already committed to the evolving human rights movement. Myron Schwartz, executive director of the Jewish Community Relations Council, spoke in support of CORE to an influential segment of the St. Louis population, including his board and member organizations. Virgil Border, director of the National Conference of Christians and Jews, rallied religious leaders and groups of educators. Schwartz, Border, and others had founded Intergroup Youth, whose objectives were to get to know others of different races and religions and to plan a large, annual, day-long interracial brotherhood conference for high school students each year. Maggie Dagen, teaching at Clayton High School, was active in the leadership of Intergroup Youth.

Leaders in the African American community, Leo Bohannon and Chester Stovall, both of the Urban League,
and David Grant, a lawyer and president of the St. Louis
chapter of the NAACP, supported CORE enthusiastically.
The United Wholesale and Distribution Workers of America, later to become the Teamsters Union, also supported
CORE. Harold Gibbons, the liberal, intellectual president
of the Teamsters, and Bernice Fisher, the young union organizer, allowed the fledgling CORE to use the union's
facilities and equipment to spread information and sometimes helped with the mailings. Other unions, church
groups, and the Metropolitan Church Federation also
gave their support. Bound by common causes, with different memberships and approaches, all were in the right
frame of mind at the right time to support CORE and its
activities for a peaceful resolution to a volatile issue. Thus,
a network of CORE supporters emerged, sharing information and ideas, to promote change.

The end of the war in 1945 had opened a window of opportunity for social change. Leaders in the religious community, including Protestants, Catholics, Jews, and members of the Ethical Society, helped bring about that change.
Prominent clergymen spoke out against segregation.
William Scarlett, the Episcopal Bishop of Missouri, was a
strong supporter of CORE. Archbishop Joseph Ritter established an open-admissions policy for Catholic parochial
schools, even though that policy was protested by some
Catholics.

And in 1947, CORE leapt into the fray, concentrating on
the opening of public accommodations. Before sit-ins and
demonstrations began, however, there were numerous in-
depth discussions of CORE's roots in the teaching and actions of Gandhi, of passive resistance, and of the absolute
verbal and physical discipline required of anyone want-

ing to be a member of the organization. Bernice Fisher had emphasized that nonviolence was not a form of weakness; rather, it was evidence of resolve and an unwillingness to meet violence with violence.

As the membership grew, the St. Louis chapter of CORE moved its meetings from the Dagens' apartment to the Centennial Christian Church at the corner of Fountain and Aubert in the city. When the group's members decided they were ready, after thorough training, they debated and decided that the initial targets should not be small facilities where food service was the primary, or only, source of income. Rather, CORE would target larger facilities such as department stores, dime stores, and drugstores where food service was only one part of the overall sales and service to customers. CORE had no desire to put any establishment out of business or cause undue financial hardship to any proprietor; CORE only wanted to change attitudes and practices. CORE wanted to achieve changes in race relations by fostering understanding, by negotiating, and, as a last resort, by direct peaceful action. It would not be easy.

Three

A Plan of Action

The informal discussions at the Dagens' resulted in an action plan, as the young people responded to Bernice Fisher's challenge. It was not a militant directive. That was neither Fisher's nor Chicago CORE's style. The St. Louis group agreed on a mission: to seek to open St. Louis's public accommodations, particularly restaurants, to African Americans. The group talked with Fisher about strategy, technique, and philosophy. Fisher addressed subsequent meetings of St. Louis CORE and maintained contact with the group until she moved from St. Louis.

Some of the first members of St. Louis CORE were ready for a challenge, ready to take on the world. Some were more timorous and remained in the background. The group had one agenda, one goal, one reason for being. Its members were determined to bring about change. But they were soon to feel the pain of prejudice that some of them had never experienced before. In restaurants and at lunch counters, as quiet protesters, they experienced embarrassment and humiliation, faced unbelievable rudeness, and risked damage to their clothing when dirty, half-filled dishes were stacked haphazardly at their places. And worse was to come. Threats were made: in one situation a counterman sharpened a knife within inches of a CORE member's throat, and on other occasions demonstrators had to dodge cups of scalding coffee or bowls of steaming soup that were shoved at them across counters.

They were ignored, laughed at, and taunted. Managers and servers whispered and cast hateful looks in their direction. But the members of CORE persisted in the strategy they had agreed upon. Each targeted eating place called for its own tailored plan, but often the same general procedure was followed:

1. A small interracial CORE team, usually two persons of the same gender, called on the owner, manager, or executive officer for a private meeting. In that meeting the CORE members requested that the eating place be opened to all. Responses varied. Seldom did this first meeting get results.

2. Without giving any kind of ultimatum, the team members asked that the idea of desegregation be considered seriously, stating that they would return for more discussion or an answer. It might require a number of meetings over a long period of time before any progress was made, but the CORE team was determined to be patient and civil, to keep the lines of communication open. Sometimes, if the two sides developed a working relationship, the manager might say: "We will serve you once a week, on Thursday, at 5 o'clock." In such cases, the number in the test group was stipulated. Team members would report faithfully at the appointed hour each week, to help ease the transition to an open-door policy. The purpose of the "test teams" was to accustom the personnel and the other diners to eating with African American customers and to observe their reactions.

3. Religious, business, and other civic leaders, sometimes as individuals, sometimes in small teams, were asked to call on management and add their support to CORE's requests that the doors be opened to all.

4. If, after all these attempts, management continued to refuse to expand service to everyone, the

CORE team stated that its only choice was to come into the restaurant, either as a two-member inter-racial team or as a group, and take seats with the other customers. This would be a test, designed to convince management that opening the doors to all would not affect white patronage and to demon-strate CORE's persistence. A CORE team would fol-low up meetings with management by going into the business and sitting at the counter or at tables wait-ing to be served, sometimes remaining for hours while being ignored or scorned by the personnel.

In the organization's first decade, members of CORE re-ported that many white customers talked pleasantly to them, either to inquire what the sit-ins were all about or to encourage them in their campaign. Seldom, if ever, did a white customer refuse to enter a restaurant where a sit-in was taking place or leave in protest. Many scarcely seemed to notice. CORE members always showed respect for the people with whom they dealt, whether they were managers or owners, employees, department store secu-rity personnel, or the city police. CORE members in-formed management and police of their plans; in turn, CORE gained their respect.

Although harsh words might be forthcoming, there were few incidents or episodes of violence. One genuine threat, however, was posed by the Christian Nationalist Crusade, a national organization founded by Gerald L. K. Smith and based in St. Louis. The Christian Nationalists promoted racist and anti-Semitic causes. Their opposition to CORE surfaced on several occasions. Christian Nation-alists harassed CORE members as they stood in line, hop-ing to integrate a cafeteria; they made threatening phone calls to CORE members late at night; and they burned a cross at the home of a CORE member. CORE members refused to be intimidated. Finally, after failing to recruit substantial support in St. Louis, Smith moved his organization's headquarters to Los Angeles.

A teenage member of the Smith movement enrolled in Maggie Dagen's high school human relations class and disagreed with opinions voiced by her and by students. "He requested a lunch hour meeting with me in a vacant school building while the other students and faculty ate in the adjacent cafeteria, and I agreed," Dagen recalled. "He got out his Christian Nationalist card, flourished a switchblade knife, and said, 'I don't suppose you know, I am a member.'"

Dagen said she was aware of his membership. She went on,

> Then I said, "I am willing to give up my lunch time to talk, but I will not do so unless you put away that knife." He put away the knife, but continued to spew forth hate language. I said, "You know, my senior class is voluntary. If you want to withdraw, I will be glad to give you a withdrawal slip." He decided to stay, but his attitudes regarding race relations did not change in a positive way. His membership and activity in the hate group continued.

During that confrontation, Dagen was not representing CORE, but she was using its approach of nonviolent, passive resistance to blunt what appeared to be a physical threat. It was rare that a CORE member had to face such threats alone or without consensus on how to handle the potentially dangerous situation. "The pooling of ideas at CORE meetings and the weighing of advantages and disadvantages of each plan helped the group work out a direction for each project, sometimes long-term and sometimes short-term," said Billie Ames Teneau. "Each week's meeting was a time for sharing what had happened since the last meeting and deciding what strategies would be used during the next week."

For several years, Billie Ames Teneau compiled the organization's newsletter, *Up to Date with CORE,* which was widely distributed, even to nonmembers of CORE. In the June 1954 issue of *Up to Date with CORE,* Ames wrote: "We in CORE have the habit of sitting in our meetings and planning as though our group were three times its actual size." In the weekly meetings, CORE members reported progress and setbacks. They reported the smallest signs that a manager or owner was beginning to yield to their persistent, quiet demands. Despite the occasional disappointment and the anger they could not show, they smiled at the ironies and ludicrous counter incidents.

Once the group agreed on the best strategy and team members took on an assignment, the team members were on their own. Maggie Dagen explained:

> We had to be very single-minded. The strategy might change from situation to situation, but we had to stay with our goals. And we might have to make a decision on the spur of the moment in response to some unexpected statement or action by the personnel. Often, we would just quietly stay there. Sometimes, we felt it was wise to leave pleasantly and calmly, and just say something like, "This may not be a good time to talk with you about this. So we will be back." We had Gandhi as a model, and the model could be described as achieving change through non-violence, physically and verbally, no matter what the provocation. You had to keep your hands to your side and a civil tongue in your mouth and be polite and courteous and, if all else failed in terms of trying to convince people quietly behind the scenes to make a change, then try to negotiate, take a more

active approach to making change. This would mean coming into an eating establishment and waiting for service, sometimes for hours. This was passive resistance.

Billie Ames Teneau added:

> I was comfortable with the non-violent philosophy. Growing up in a family where voices were never raised in anger and punishments were the result of rational reasoning, the non-violent approach seemed to be the only approach.
>
> Time was spent in the meetings discussing how members should respond when faced with anger or violence. Our conclusions were very much in the "respond to bad with good" category. Be nice, no matter what. Be kind, but do not be weak. Do not give in unless it is strategically wise to do so. All this fit in very well with my upbringing and my Methodist background.

CORE instilled this philosophy in its members from the very beginning with frequent training sessions. As new people came into CORE, if they could not accept and practice these disciplines, or if they tried to mix other agendas or ideologies, political or religious, with CORE's agenda, they were told that they could not participate. It quickly became clear to such individuals that to be involved, they had to meet CORE's criteria.

Discussions and decisions within CORE were friendly and nonconfrontational, although everyone was urged to speak up until consensus was reached. At weekly meetings, first at the Dagens' apartment and later in the basement of the Christian Centennial Church, the group based its decisions on consensus, not on formal votes.

"Because many initial CORE members had participated in other organizations, as students, employees, or volunteers, and were of like minds on race discrimination," said Irv Dagen, "it was easy to have a meeting of the minds on philosophy and plans for action as described by Bernice Fisher."

"CORE had to have an impact on what people became and on how they thought in a group and how they thought independently and how nonthreatening it was to disagree with one another," said Maggie Dagen. "We often had a short session about CORE discipline and if someone was wobbling a bit, or feeling uneasy about being able to withstand insults or frustration, we would talk about it. As new people came in we had training sessions exclusively for them, sometimes role playing."

Rules were strict and reflected the group's Gandhian philosophy of nonviolence. Rules given out to new members included

> ATTITUDES AND CONDUCT: We do not partic-
> ipate in picket lines because we hate the manager or
> the employees for discriminating against colored
> people. We have picket lines because we want the
> manager and employees to change their attitude to-
> ward Negroes and treat everyone equally. We can-
> not accomplish this by becoming angry ourselves. If
> anyone—manager, employee or passer-by—speaks
> to you unkindly or even shoves you, do not show
> any anger. To do so would simply result in the other
> person giving additional displays of his anger. . . .
> POLICE: The police have been notified by CORE
> that the demonstration is going to take place. If a po-
> liceman asks you something about the demonstra-
> tion, refer him to the demonstration leader. If you are
> asked for your name and address, don't hesitate to
> give them to the police—we have nothing to hide.

No participant knew what the next visit to a targeted eating place might bring. It would be months, or even

CORE PRECEDENT SHEET
PICKET LINES

This precedent sheet will give you the general rules which CORE people have found advantageous during past CORE picket lines.

COURTESY: In addition to being courteous to customers, managers, and passers-by, we try to be courteous to each other. If you agree to arrive at a certain place at a particularly time or do something at an appointed time, try to keep your word. Be prompt. We are all busy people.

APPEARANCE: Try to have a neat clean appearance. This becomes very difficult when the temperature gets to about 104 degrees, but do the best you can.

ATTITUDES AND CONDUCT: We do not participate in picket lines because we hate the manager or the employees for discriminating against colored people. We have picket lines because we want the manager and employees to change their attitude toward Negroes and treat everyone equally. We cannot accomplish this by becoming angry ourselves. If anyone--manager, employee or passer-by--speaks to you unkindly or even shoves you, do not show any anger. To do so would simply result in the other person giving additional displays of his anger.

If someone should direct his anger at you, either ignor him or (in case you have been shoved) excuse yourself for having been in his way. Then continue passing out leaflets, walking in the picket line or doing whatever you were before the person arrived.

DEMONSTRATION LEADER: Some one or two CORE members are in charge of every CORE demonstration. When arriving at the place for the picket line, report to the leader of the demonstration before participating. If you don't know who is in charge, ask someone already participating. no what the leader asks you to. He will circulate among the demonstrators, will have an over-all view of what is going on and will be in the best position to know where your participation can do the most good. if you have any criticisms as to how the demonstration is being run, bring them up at the next meeting.

If at any time, you feel that you cannot continue participating in the demonstration, tell the demonstration leader before leaving. It may be necessary for you to leave if someone angers you to such an extent that you feel you may not be able to maintain a peaceful attitude, if you feel ill, or perhaps for some other reason.

QUESTIONS: CORE people are frequently asked many questions by employees and passers-by. Some of these may be malicious questions, some may come from a sincere desire to know more about our organization and what we are doing. Answer all questions truthfully and courteously. If you do not know the answers, refer the person to the demonstration leader or to one of the regular CORE members.

POLICE: The police have been notified by CORE that the demonstration is going to take place. If a policeman asks you something about the demonstration, refer him to the demonstration leader. If you are asked for your name and address, don't hesitate to give them to the police--we have nothing to hide.

Handout prepared by St. Louis CORE for members preparing to picket.

years, before they could count their successes. Today, the activists, grown a half century older, remember CORE for what it was: a worthy undertaking with headaches, heartaches, and successes. A major beneficial outcome was the creation of mutual support and friendship among erstwhile adversaries.

Four

A Case Study: Shop Here but Do Not Eat Here

When CORE was born in 1947, downtown St. Louis was flourishing. It was a center of retail establishments with three major department stores, exclusive specialty shops, chain stores, dime stores, and drugstores. It had hotels, restaurants, small cafes, cafeterias, and theaters. It had banks, investment firms, professional offices, and federal and city government offices and courts. It was where the major St. Louis action occurred. The streets were crowded. Traffic police stood at major intersections, waving their arms and blowing their whistles to direct motorists and assist pedestrians. Shoppers and store and office workers crowded the sidewalks until it was sometimes difficult to walk through the throng.

Thousands of workers, shoppers, and visitors arrived downtown via streetcars clanging east and west down Market, Olive, Pine, and Washington and across Broadway and other north-south streets from Twelfth (now Tucker Boulevard) eastward to the river. The streetcars ran every ten minutes on the main lines. People could also travel downtown by bus or in "service cars," big automobiles that could accommodate six or seven passengers, and, for a higher fare, would take passengers all the way to the University City Loop or to quiet Clayton, the county seat.

At the western and northern edges of the downtown business and shopping district, bounded by Market, Delmar, Twelfth, and Broadway, were clothing and hat manufacturers, national shoe companies, wholesale dry goods establishments, warehouses, and the major newspapers' offices. Downtown St. Louis housed the first-run movie theaters, the Ambassador, the Fox, and Loew's State Theater, and also live theater, the American and the Orpheum. There were burlesque houses; concerts could be heard at Kiel Opera House; and conventions and sporting events took place at Kiel Auditorium. Three daily newspapers, the *St. Louis Globe Democrat,* the *St. Louis Post-Dispatch,* and the *St. Louis Star Times,* informed the region from downtown. The YMCA, the YWCA, and major churches also served downtown St. Louis. The National Park Service had acquired the land along the Mississippi River and had begun to clear the old riverfront commercial district in 1939, but the Jefferson National Expansion Memorial Park was still a dream, and the St. Louis Arch had not even been imagined.

Businessmen met for luncheons at major hotel dining rooms and private clubs. Stores closed at 5 P.M., except during the busy holiday season, but workers stayed downtown and suburbanites rode the streetcars in to dine or attend movies or plays. Parades attracted thousands of people from all parts of the metropolitan area.

There were three large department stores: Famous-Barr; Scruggs, Vandervoort, Barney; and Stix, Baer & Fuller; each occupied a full block and rose six to nine floors. Their window displays attracted shoppers during the day and window shoppers after hours, as did the windows of the smaller, fashionable retailers: Kline's, Garland's, Sonnenfeld's, Cunningham's, Best & Co., and Peck and Peck. Mermod, Jaccard, & King and Hess & Culbertson sold fine jewelry; Peacock's and Swope's sold shoes; and Leppert Roos sold furs. During the Christmas season, families poured into the heart of the city to enjoy the animated Christmas windows and to shop. Saturdays and holidays were shopping excursion days.

The population of the St. Louis metropolitan area was concentrated within the city limits and nearby suburbs. White flight and westward expansion, and the suburban sprawl that would accompany them, had not yet occurred. Except for older communities such as Kirkwood, Webster Groves, University City, Wellston, Florissant, Ferguson, and Clayton, much of the county was still farmland with sparse residential development. Even Clayton, the county seat, had the leisurely ambiance of a small Missouri town. It still had taverns, small shops, a family-owned hardware store, and general stores where you could buy overalls, oil lamps, and coils of rope.

In 1950 the city of St. Louis had a population of more than 850,000. By 1997 the population was less than 350,000, fewer than the total number of workers, shoppers, and visitors who had thronged the downtown area in 1950. At midcentury, downtown was busy and prosperous, the heart of a metropolis with a glorious heritage and an exhilarating future.

In a guest commentary in the *St. Louis Post-Dispatch,* February 16, 1997, Robert Archibald, president of the Missouri Historical Society, looked back on that time:

> The city and its downtown, despite historical inequities and failures, were places where we intermingled, places that imbued their citizens with a sense of civic undertaking and a conviction that we are interdependent, with mutual obligations, with a past we shared and, implicitly, a future.
>
> It was the place where we came face-to-face on a regular basis with people with whom we share this spot on the planet. It was the place that could make us realize that to get along we must be civil and observe common standards of behavior and that we must accept a shared responsibility for the health and welfare of the civic enterprise.

During the time he was recalling, fifty years ago, St. Louis had been a thriving, hopeful city. But its black citizens had suffered the privations and indignities of racial segregation. African Americans worked in service jobs and as unskilled labor, rarely in production jobs. Few worked in offices, retailing, skilled crafts, or building trades. Postal service and other government jobs open to blacks were highly prized. Theaters were segregated, although public transportation was not. Downtown hotels, restaurants, cafeterias, and lunch counters did not serve African Americans.

So CORE, observing what thousands were too blind to see, went to work. In 1948 CORE chose Stix, Baer & Fuller, a major department store with a large, first-floor, sit-down lunch counter, for a comprehensive, direct-action effort. The choice of Stix, Baer & Fuller, known in earlier days as the "Grand Leader," did not reflect an attempt to focus on discrimination in just one store. In fact, CORE was working simultaneously with executives of Famous-Barr and Scruggs, Vandervoort, Barney, and managers of eating facilities in Woolworth's and other chain dime stores, Walgreen's and other chain drugstores (all with lunch counters), and various chain and independent cafeterias. CORE used an individually designed strategy for each time and place. The Stix experience was special because there CORE members employed many strategies and creative variations of strategies. Stix became, in a sense, a CORE case study. CORE chose Stix for a comprehensive, direct-action effort for the following reasons:

*Stix was owned by St. Louisans who were leaders in the civic and cultural life of the community.
*As members of the establishment and leaders in retailing, the officers of Stix could be expected to re-

spond to pressure from community, religious, and other organizations and from customers.

*Its large, first-floor lunch counter would provide visibility for CORE's efforts.

*Its lunch counter was a service to customers but did not account for a large percentage of operating revenues.

The December 1951 issue of *Up to Date with CORE* contains a chronology of events that took place at Stix from mid–1948 to December 1951. It recounts the long, difficult effort that utilized direct-action sit-ins, and it tells of CORE's decision to discontinue sit-ins at Stix while instituting them at Famous-Barr and at dime stores and drugstores. This pulling back was part of an overall strategy designed to give Stix an opportunity to voluntarily open the lunch counter while saving face. The strategy paid off; Stix voluntarily opened its first-floor eating facilities in 1954.

It is clear from these records that the earliest talks with Stix officials in 1948 were unsuccessful. When follow-up letters went unanswered, CORE began distributing leaflets outside the store. The first flyers depicted a baseball player under the heading "All We Ask Is Fair Play." The flyers explained that African Americans were being denied service and urged customers to complain to the management.

In September, new leaflets were distributed. These displayed a picture of a drum majorette under the heading "The Grand Leader—in Everything but Democracy" and again asked customers to complain. Later leaflets ran a picture of the Statue of Liberty and asked, "Does the Declaration of Independence read like this? 'We hold these truths to be self-evident, all men, *except Negroes,* are created equal.'"

In October, continuing the information campaign, CORE distributed leaflets that showed a picture of a judge and addressed the recipient with the words, "You be the judge: Is it fair to refuse restaurant service to Negroes while accepting money from them in other departments?" Leaflets were dropped from an airplane as well as distributed by members on the ground. Unfortunately, many of those dropped landed on rooftops or in the river. But the old-fashioned, person-to-person, on-the-ground campaign continued without interruption.

CORE took advantage of every opportunity to get its message across with creative, specially tailored methods. In November 1948, when an ecumenical association met on the ninth floor of Stix, CORE distributed leaflets that showed two faces and asked, "Who is the boss of Stix? Is he the man who entertains liberal groups on the ninth floor? Or is he the man who won't permit minority groups to meet in his first-floor restaurant? Ask the managers to practice what they preach."

On January 28, 1949, a year after CORE representatives first met with executives at Stix, a member of CORE wrote to the company president, pointing out that "on two recent occasions when several Negroes remained seated several hours after being refused service, customers continued to sit next to the colored CORE members and eat."

A few days later, two white members went to the lunch counter, sat down, and ordered four hamburgers. After they were served, four black CORE members sat down with them and shared the hamburgers. The white CORE members then ordered pie, which they intended to share with the blacks. After the pie was ordered, the manager put a "closed" sign on the counter. At several small CORE sit-ins that followed, "closed" signs were placed at each section of the counter where a black was seated, but the undaunted demonstrators stayed in place for several hours.

To support its contention that white customers did not object to sharing the restaurant with black customers, CORE wrote to top executives on April 12, 1949, stating that when blacks sat at the counter, "white customers continued to sit at the counter and eat, even sitting in seats next to the Negroes. . . . We like to have policy changes take place quietly, but a lack of co-operation left us with no alternative but to appeal to the public through public demonstrations."

When there was no response to that letter, CORE demonstrations became weekly events, with an average of twenty to thirty people occupying places in the ninety-seven–seat facility. One Saturday, fifty-seven CORE people sat at the first-floor counter all day. Demonstrators remained quietly from 10 A.M. to 4:30 P.M. on Saturday, and from 4:30 to 8 P.M. Monday. At first, they sat next to one another. Later, they changed strategy to occupy every other seat. White customers would sit between them and be served. CORE members placed small signs on the counter before them: "We are Being Refused Service," along with explanatory leaflets.

"Strategies to attract attention to our demonstrations took many forms," Billie Ames Teneau recalled. "At one sit-in demonstration, a black member sat at a restaurant counter with a large sign on his back reading, 'We have been waiting for service ___ hours and ___ minutes.' The time was changed every 15 minutes. There were always several customers reading the sign, including one supposed 'blind' man complete with cup and cane!"

A photographer from the *St. Louis American,* a weekly newspaper serving the African American community, was on hand when Billie Ames and Connie Williams tried to lunch together at Stix. Billie recalled the incident:

> When my son Greg was nine and a half months old, the two of us sat at the lunch counter at Stix, Baer & Fuller, alongside the somewhat darker-hued Connie Williams and her daughter, Vicky Lynn, 10 months old. As a part of a CORE sit-in demonstration, we did attract some attention though the waitresses and customers said very little to us.
>
> The *St. Louis American,* on May 12, 1949, printed a front-page picture of us with our children standing outside the store. The headline read, "Two Mothers Repulsed by Unlifted Blockage at S.B.F. store." The article added that the store management stated that the non service was a matter of "public policy."
>
> "Mrs Ames could have been served if she had not insisted on eating with her friend, Mrs. Williams. . . . They are protesting for an American way that practices what it preaches to the world."

Walter Hayes, another member, remembered:

> A CORE incident that I cherish, was sitting at Stix, Baer & Fuller's first-floor restaurant—a huge place with many, many seats. There never seemed to me to be enough CORE members at that time to make much of an impact on filling the seats and disrupting business, one of our tactics being to occupy seats so that no one could sit there to eat and spend money.
>
> One day a CORE member got up from his seat for a few minutes and left his Bible, which I was reading, open on the counter. When customers came in to eat, amazingly, none of them would sit within five or six seats of that open Bible. The next day, we all brought Bibles and spread them throughout the cafeteria. With only a few people and several Bibles we almost shut the place down.

Connie Williams with daughter, Vicky Lynn, and Billie Ames with son, Gregory, in front of Stix, Baer & Fuller after being refused service at the department store's lunch counter, May 12, 1949. Reprinted by permission of the *St. Louis American*.

During one of the demonstrations, Stix employees were instructed to occupy all the vacant seats in the long front section. "They sat there for several hours reading magazines," reported *Up to Date with CORE*. "Stix soon realized that this was only helping us and discontinued the sit-in by their employees."

Starting in May 1949, leaflets were frequently distributed to people outside the store while the sit-ins were going on inside. After reading the leaflets, many people did not go into the building. Those who did frequently stood outside the railing that enclosed the first-floor eating counter and watched, causing a great deal of congestion in the aisle and considerable concern to management.

Individual CORE members added strength to the group effort with their own protests. Marian O'Fallon Oldham received a letter from Stix advertising a policy whereby teachers could buy clothing during the summer and pay in the fall. Oldham took the letter to the store and explained she could not participate in the plan because of the racial discrimination practiced at the first-floor lunch counter. The man she spoke with expressed surprise at her decision. He seemed not to understand her feelings and explained that there was no discrimination in the credit department. But CORE's struggle to make people aware of such hypocritical behavior was having an effect. Public interest was increasing, and many individuals closed their Stix charge accounts in support of the effort to open eating facilities.

During a Missouri American Legion convention in St. Louis, Stix placed advertisements in the daily newspapers welcoming the delegates and inviting them to visit the store. CORE arranged for several African American Legionnaires to answer the advertisement by visiting the first-floor lunch counter. *Up to Date with CORE* reported:

> When they were refused service, two of them went upstairs to complain to the manager and the other two joined the CORE demonstration. Other customers were disturbed because the Legionnaires were not served. Some customers attempted to buy food for them, and did buy food for some of the CORE members.

This incident was headlined in the *St. Louis American*, and five hundred copies of the newspaper, along with leaflets urging readers to boycott Stix, were distributed outside the store.

In 1949 reinforcements for CORE's ranks arrived. Southern students traveled to St. Louis to do summer social service work under the auspices of the Association of Southern Churches. Ten of the students, who were white, attended CORE meetings and then joined the demonstrations at Stix, ordering, being served, and then passing the food to black CORE members.

CORE urged Stix customers to boycott the store, concentrating its efforts on the African American community. On August 29, 1949, the NAACP passed a resolution calling for a citywide boycott of Stix. Church and civic groups aided CORE by allowing CORE speakers to explain the boycott to their members. Many individuals wrote letters and made phone calls urging others to observe the boycott.

When none of these actions broke the store's color barrier in its first-floor eating facility, CORE decided on another strategy. On July 28, 1949, a letter to store executives asked that they meet with members of CORE to decide on a specific date, three or four weeks hence, to end discrimination. During the waiting period, CORE would discontinue demonstrations. Then, on the opening day, two or three blacks would eat at the counter without fanfare or publicity. Small groups would continue to eat there until it became generally accepted that it was open to African Americans. The letter was not answered.

After sixteen months of peaceful negotiations and nonviolent protests, CORE members discontinued the demonstrations "to give Stix a chance to change policy and save face at the same time," according to the article in *Up to Date with CORE*. In a letter to Stix's president, CORE pointed out that its demonstrations had proved the willingness of customers to share the counter with blacks. In fact, the overwhelming majority of customers had stated that blacks should be served. "Now," the letter continued, "CORE will discontinue demonstrations so that Stix can make the change while no public attention is being called to the situation."

But the story did not end there. CORE's struggle was based on an underlying philosophy of goodwill, negotiation, reconciliation with adversaries, and peaceful direct action. Cessation of the sit-in demonstrations was not a surrender; rather, it was a regrouping. On November 31, 1951, Walter Hayes and Charles Oldham met with Stix officials to fill them in on CORE's successes in opening some of the leading dime store and drugstore chains and to inform them of testing underway at other eating facilities. As in earlier discussions, there was a civil give-and-take, but the Stix managers refused to open their counter.

As discussions continued with management of Famous-Barr and Scruggs, as well as with managers of other eating establishments, CORE developed a new approach. In April 1952, Charles Oldham, then president of CORE, worked with other members to prepare "A Plan for Establishing Equal Restaurant Service in St. Louis Department Stores." The four-point proposal recommended a timetable for prearranged eating tests by small interracial groups at three department stores. The proposal promised that there would be no newspaper publicity about the tests during their execution. The proposal was also sent to community leaders, and their response was swift and positive.

Dr. Ruth M. Harris, president of Stowe Teachers College and member of the St. Louis Council on Human Relations, wrote: "Your plan . . . seems to me to be very well planned. At this moment I can think of no better procedure, and so, wish to give hearty support of it and to offer my assistance for carrying out this program."

Dr. C. Oscar Johnson, minister of the Third Baptist Church, wrote: "I believe that the plan is sound. I am sure that there can be no objection on the part of fair-minded people for the thing you are trying to do. . . . I, personally, feel very much in favor of it and I would like very much to see the experiment given a try."

And from the Reverend Albert S. Foley, S.J., professor of sociology at Saint Louis University, came this endorsement: "The plan . . . seems to be a logical and ineluctable next step in St. Louis's steady progress toward the fulfillment of our American ideal of freedom of access to American opportunities and facilities."

Representative Claude I. Bakewell, the Republican congressman from Missouri's eleventh district, wrote from Washington: "It appears utterly inconsistent that the department stores would welcome the patronage of a large segment of the population at all counters and in all departments but would arbitrarily exclude them from the dining facilities."

Many others added their endorsements, including Mrs. E. V. Cowdry of the St. Louis Council on Human Relations; Chester E. Stovall, director of Industrial Relations for the Urban League of Metropolitan St. Louis; the Reverend James W. Clarke, minister of the Second Presbyterian Church and president of the St. Louis Metropolitan Church Federation; Ellsworth J. Evans, president of the Catholic Interracial Council; the Reverend W. Elbert Starn, executive secretary of the Disciples of Christ of Greater St. Louis; R. L. Witherspoon, attorney and member of the legal redress committee and executive committee of the St. Louis NAACP; Niels C. Beck, member of the Catholic Interracial Council; and M. Leo Bohannon, executive director of the Urban League of Metropolitan St. Louis.

By the end of 1952, some stores were still in the negotiating mode, some had permitted "testing," and some had actually opened their doors. Although CORE's 1952 "Plan for Establishing Equal Restaurant Service in St. Louis Department Stores" was not adopted by the stores, it did reach their inner management and executive circles. CORE also sent the stores a portfolio of the supportive letters from civic and religious leaders. Stix's policy remained unchanged throughout 1953, but the next year, without a word to CORE and with no public notice, the Grand Leader opened its counter to all.

It was a partial victory. As reported in *Up to Date with CORE*, Billie Ames telephoned the store to commend the policy change. Billie asked about the Humpty Dumpty and the Missouri Room Restaurants and was told that "the policies of these places have not changed." That would come much later. But the CORE battle with Stix, at the first-floor level, was over at last. The patient, persistent CORE approach had prevailed. Word came back that the top department store personnel had been impressed by CORE's approach. CORE's battle plan continued to succeed throughout the city. More establishments opened their doors, and in 1961 the St. Louis Board of Aldermen passed a public accommodations ordinance requiring such facilities to be open to all without discrimination.

Five

Dime Stores, Drugstores, CORE

During a CORE demonstration at Woolworth's a by-
stander asked Raul deLoayza if he was a Mexican,
an Indian, a Negro, or what; and Raul replied, "I'm a
man."

Up to Date with CORE, September 1951

When CORE began its demonstrations in 1947, "five-
and-dime" variety stores such as Woolworth's, Kresge's,
and Neisner's dotted the downtown as well as outlying
neighborhoods. In addition to their inexpensive merchandise, most offered food service. Many chain and independent drugstores, too, served sandwiches and other
foods, along with malts, shakes, and sundaes, at their
soda fountains. The old five-and-dimes and the corner
drugstores gradually gave way to major drug chains, and
in this cultural transition, lunch counters and soda fountains, American icons, disappeared. But in the dime
stores' and drugstores' heyday, thousands of workers and
shoppers, especially those in the downtown area, made
these counters their regular noonday stop. Because
African Americans were not permitted to sit down at
these counters, although at some places they could stand
and be served, CORE targeted these stores in the months
and years of their demonstrations on behalf of racial
equality.

When chains began to replace the independent mer-
chants, CORE adopted the tactic of negotiating with regional or even national officers who had more authority

and might be more inclined than local managers to change policy. An outstanding example of CORE's persuasiveness can be found in the story of the Woolworth's campaign. In July 1950, Irv Dagen, St. Louis CORE's primary negotiator with Woolworth's management, wrote for an article in *CORE-lator*, the publication of national CORE, that the store's managers in St. Louis had been "almost unanimously unfriendly."

In a 1995 taped interview Dagen elaborated:

> The whole idea of CORE from the beginning was to win over to our way of thinking people who, initially, for good or bad reasons, were opposed to some of the things we were trying to accomplish. Woolworth's offers a prime example.
>
> They had a store in downtown St. Louis which was then a more active city than it is now, with respect to retail: department stores, dime stores. There were any number of dime stores, but they aren't around any more. The downtown Woolworth's had a stand-up counter and a sit-down counter. Blacks could stand up, couldn't sit down. It was what Harry Golden, the North Carolina humorist and civil rights champion, called "vertical integration."
>
> Within a short time I got to meet Mr. Breland, the southwest regional manager. I talked to him and said it doesn't make any sense. He could see my point of view, but he was not certain that change could be brought about.
>
> Woolworth's had a store in north St. Louis, in a totally black neighborhood, and we decided to have a picket line, people marching up and down, distributing leaflets and saying something to the effect of "Don't feed Jim Crow." We were convincing and nobody bought anything. If you know anything about chain stores, they keep tabs on everything. They're not going to go broke. It's just the idea that something is wrong.

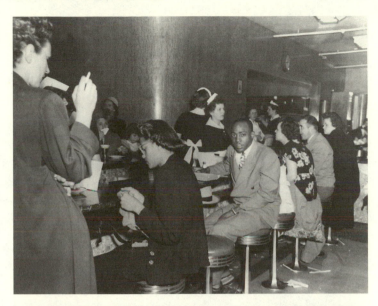

Mary McClain and Willie Collins, Jr., at a CORE sit-in at the downtown Woolworth's lunch counter in the late 1940s. Reprinted by permission of the *St. Louis American*.

> There is always a peculiar excuse on the part of management that the employees wouldn't go along. The general response we made, in a nonviolent way, was, "Since when do you go along with your employees?"

Dagen's efforts finally paid off after many months, not only opening doors, but creating goodwill and forging a friendship with an erstwhile opponent:

> We became good friends and met at various times to talk about this problem. He told me that hereafter there would not be another Woolworth's store opened in the Southwestern region without having it be open to everybody who came in. So it seemed

to me a pretty good, I won't call it conversion, but certainly convincing and making a friend out of somebody who potentially was an enemy. This was the philosophy we had.

When he was president of national CORE, Charles Old-ham had a similar experience with the same store official:

> I remember when I was in New Orleans one time and Mr. Breland was there and I met with him because the New Orleans CORE was actively demonstrating.
>
> I met with him at his hotel. We had a long talk and he was very complimentary toward Irv Dagen. He had a good deal of admiration for him and, as a result of that, we were able to work out a situation involving the New Orleans CORE group which ended up, in about three or four months, in the opening of those facilities.

However, victory had not been won without persistent, patient effort. In 1995, Irene Williams wrote from Sitka, Alaska: "My experience at the Woolworth store on Grand and Olive remains outstanding in my mind, because I did it alone." Irene, a CORE member, was a student of speech and language therapy at St. Louis University in 1953 when she was refused service at a nearby Woolworth's. CORE arranged with the manager that she carry out a test. The manager assigned her a stool at the end of the serving counter where she was to sit when she came in on Wednesdays around noon:

> The seat that I had been assigned happened to be right in front of the coffee urn, the soup pot and the knife sharpener.... One of the counter women shoved a cup of hot coffee in my direction and I dodged just in time to keep it from landing in my

lap.... It landed on the floor and remained there until I left.

Soup was splattered around the area and I became very much aware of huge, dangerous looking knives being sharpened and slid across the counter.

Most of the women behind the counter were ... unflinchingly mean-spirited toward me.... Yet there was one gentle soul who frequently shoved a bowl of soup toward me and smiled benignly.... I made an effort to eat it but had a hard time because I think it was soup that someone else had returned.

After about two months one of the women behind the counter asked me if I wanted to order anything. I said no for two reasons: one was that I never had expected to have the opportunity to order and the other was that I was so sure I would not that I didn't even take my purse inside but left it in the car.

After that, I was always given the opportunity to order and I always did so. The manager then informed me that I could sit wherever I wanted. This was really good news. Near the end of the semester he met me at the door and said the sit-in was no longer necessary because he was opening the entire store to everyone. I think he even smiled. I know I did, broadly. He shook my hand and said, "You did a good job."

Another important CORE effort was centered on Katz Drug Store. In the early 1950s, Katz Drug Company, headquartered in Kansas City, Missouri, was a major retail establishment in downtown St. Louis, as well as in outlying neighborhoods. The continuing CORE-Katz story was reported in *Up to Date with CORE.* One of the most dramatic chapters occurred on Saturday, October 28, 1950. If it had not been so serious, it might have reminded onlookers of a Keystone Kops movie. CORE's tactics, peaceful but well orchestrated, undoubtedly frustrated management and employees. It began this way:

Augustus Bell and Joe Ames sat at the counter in the Katz store at 8th and Washington, at 10:10 am. No one took their order. The manager of the food department . . . said to a customer, in a loud voice, "I don't like having that SOB at my counter."

At 10:45 other CORE people began coming in in twos and threes. The manager of the food department sat next to Joe and very belligerently asked if there was anything Joe had to say to him. Joe explained why we were there. The manager suggested we talk with Mr. Francis, his superior, and write letters to the Katz headquarters in Kansas City.

Two black CORE members, Bill Ingram and Marian O'Fallon, came in and sat at the counter. Two white members, Marvin Rich and Don Hunstein, sat in a booth and were served. Don got up and Bill sat down and ate the food. Charles Oldham and Martha Rudner, both white, were served in a booth. Charlie gave Marian O'Fallon his seat and Marian ate the food. As other CORE members sat at the counter, all counter service stopped.

Shortly after noon, the manager started allowing only people he okayed to be served. At least 30 customers were told they could not be served. Many others were permitted to sit but left because of the poor service.

Rose and Jerry Parnas were served in a booth. Jerry traded places with Marian Givens. The waitress grabbed part of the food and took it back to the kitchen. The bill was for the full amount.

Sandy Brent and Eleanor Smith were served in a booth. Sandy gave Gwendolyn Givens his place. A waitress grabbed Gwendolyn's plate and threw it into a metal receptacle, smashing it. Then she tore up Gwen's check.

The manager studied Sally Heller for a while and then decided she could be served. After Sally was served, Allyce Stewart joined her. The manager snatched the food away, saying, "These dishes are dirty." Throughout the day, most of the employees

talked about "niggers," "nigger-lovers," and "nig-
ger-loving Jews."

As the group left at 3 o'clock, Joe Ames told the
manager that he hoped he realized this had not been
a personal thing with CORE, and the manager apparently took it all in a friendly spirit.

Maggie Dagen recalled another dramatic encounter at
Katz during a Christmas holiday season. She and Wanda
Penny were put to a true test of their internal fortitude.
They sat down at the counter, waiting to be served, and as
Maggie remembered,

> The manager had his people pile dirty dishes, ooz-
> ing with turkey and dressing and gravy and cran-
> berry sauce, in front of us until they were ready to
> fall over. I had a *New York Times* and I said quietly to
> Wanda, "I think we had better put this on our laps,
> because I think we are going to get pretty messed up
> here."
>
> Seeing that this didn't drive us away, the manag-
> er had the dishes cleared and then leaned way over
> the counter. He was a short man, and he had a knife
> with a blade about eight or ten inches long, and he
> sharpened it right at my neck, under my Adam's ap-
> ple. My hands got wet. I was nervous, but I didn't
> pull back, and I didn't move. So he quit doing that.
>
> Wanda was absolutely staunch.

But Maggie Dagen was not willing to let such treatment
of Wanda and herself, or of any other CORE member, go
unchallenged. When she was scheduled to attend a teachers' meeting in Kansas City, she made an appointment to
see Earl Katz, head of the company.

> He did not ask me to sit down, so I stood on one side
> of his desk for an hour and talked. Finally he said,
> "You may sit down."

My pitch was that they let Wanda and me, or any other interracial two, come in on a regular basis every week and be served. And that would lead to opening the store. He was worried about publicity, but I said, "The daily newspapers haven't touched us." And I promised we would keep it out of the black newspapers.

Finally he agreed. And I said, "I have to tell you something, very honestly. You've lost. We are not going to come in there once or twice a week for the next five years on this basis. It's got to open up altogether. We'll go along for a test period, but you've lost, putting it on those terms."

He said, "O.K. We want regular reports from you."

We came back, and the same hostile manager had been told to serve us, and he wasn't very happy about it. And we never got much of a smile out of him. But I made regular reports by telephone, and when Mr. Katz came to town, he stayed at the Chase, and he would call. After a period of time, every time he came to town, he would say, "Why don't you and Irv come down and have a drink with me?" We would drop everything to see him, and we became very good friends.

Out of this eventually emerged the same thing that Irv said about Mr. Breland and Woolworth's. Katz had a southwest region which included Missouri, Kansas, Oklahoma and maybe a part of Texas. And they never again set up a segregated facility.

R. E. Neal, the manager of Neisner's Dime Store, at 521 Washington Avenue, was a very angry man when Irv Dagen and Walter Hayes first encountered him on December 17, 1949. However, he became one of the many who ultimately were won over. According to an account in *Up to Date with CORE,*

Irv and Walter sat down at the lunch counter. A waitress called Mr. Neal, who told Irv and Walter to get out of the store before he cracked their heads. Walter smiled at Mr. Neal in a very friendly manner. Mr. Neal put his hand on Walter's head and his fist in Walter's face and said, "Boy, don't you laugh at me." Then he called Irv and Walter "Communists" and said he'd kick them all the way to Moscow. He added that he was the toughest Irishman in St. Louis.

Then Mr. Neal tried to get Walter to believe that Irv was getting paid to work for CORE. He told Irv that he ought to be ashamed of himself for trying to agitate and stir up trouble. Then Mr. Neal said that if the CORE members were not out of the store in five minutes he was going to fire his colored employees.

During Mr. Neal's outburst, Irv and Walter maintained a calm attitude of goodwill. Finally, Mr. Neal calmed down and agreed to open the eating facilities in his store if the other dime stores opened theirs. He said he would like to come to one of our meetings. . . . Mr. Neal attended three managerial meetings arranged by CORE.

In August 1951, *Up to Date with CORE* reported success at Neisner's. "Test groups have been given good service for about a year now, because of Mr. Neal's friendly, cooperative attitude." Remembering the Neisner experience, Irv Dagen said of Neal:

> He began to see that there was reason to what we were proposing, that it could be done without any upheaval to his work force or his customers, and he began to understand what we were trying to do. I don't think he would have gone out and done the same thing himself without our testing and negotiating, but he was willing to concede that we had a point, and he was willing to be friendly. He moved along with us.

On April 30, 1951, things at Kresge's were far from friendly. In fact, the situation became ominous when the manager threatened to fire Negro employees as a result of CORE's demonstration. An account in *Up to Date with CORE* read:

> The demonstration started at 5 P.M. Shortly after the group arrived, Joe Ames was called aside by Mr. Carter and another store official. With a great deal of profanity, the store official asked Joe how old he was, where he worked, what he learned in "American-ism" classes at school, had he been in the army, etc.
>
> Then after boasting about their company's contributions to Negro welfare agencies, the two officials threatened to fire all their 59 Negro employees if the CORE group did not leave. Joe listened peacefully, then rejoined the demonstration.

The Kresge's officials did not realize that they had been talking to a Purple Heart veteran, a man who had lost his leg in combat and after the war had attended Washington University, where he became active in the American Veterans Committee and in SCAN, and now was demonstrating for the rights of all in St. Louis to be served in dime stores, drugstores, and restaurants. While he remained calm, some of the black Kresge employees were worried. One told Walter Hayes that he would get fired if CORE did not leave. Walter assured the busboy that he would not get fired; if he did, Walter would find him another job.

The account in *Up to Date with CORE* continued:

> At 5:45, all the colored employees were called upstairs by Mr. Schoonover. Joe telephoned Bennie Rodgers, assistant editor of the *St. Louis American* and asked him to come down to Kresge's. Joe also contacted the three daily newspapers and Mr. Howard Woods, city editor of the *St. Louis Argus.* . . .
> Mr. Rodgers phoned the store manager, who said he knew nothing about any firings.

> About 6 pm, a colored waitress talked to Walter and said she was going to lose her job if the CORE group did not leave, and that their checks were being made right then. Walter assured her it was just a bluff.

Then, as now, the *St. Louis American* and the *St. Louis Argus* were powerful voices in the St. Louis black community, often carrying important stories that the daily press ignored or downplayed. For several years, beginning in 1949, Irv Dagen wrote a regular column for the *St. Louis Argus* in which he frequently discussed CORE activities. Both papers staunchly supported CORE, and that was evident in the quick response of black journalists on the night of the Kresge incident. According to *Up to Date with CORE:*

> Mr. Rodgers of the *American* arrived at Kresge's and one of the busboys took him to the room where Mr. Schoonover and three other store officials were talking with the colored employees. . . . Mr. Schoonover told Mr. Rodgers that no one was going to be fired but that they would be transferred to other departments. He said he was going to close the food section.
>
> By 6:30 P.M., all the eating facilities in the store were closed, about 225 seats. The CORE group continued sitting until 7:30 P.M. and then left. Mr. Woods of the *Argus* told about the incident on his radio program at 9:30 P.M. that night.
>
> The day after the demonstration, the food department was serving again.

Kresge's did not fire anyone, nor were African American employees fired at other establishments where CORE demonstrated. Further efforts to intimidate CORE members also failed. But for all its successes, CORE sometimes

For Human Rights

by Irvin Dagen

AH, love, what to do on Saturday? CORE members are all Saturday's children . . . working all week long for pay . . .but come Saturday they work for love. Like what happened to this one on Saturday, December 17, S-day at Stix.

Billie Ames called him Friday nite, needed a ride to take baby Greg to Mervene Ross' house on Saturday morning, so Mervene's mother could watch Greg while Billie went to Stix to sit. Billie lives in Overland, Mervene in Brentwood and the driver in U. City, so he was up and out in the still dark of the morning, spick and span as all CORE members who go on display each Saturday at Stix. After a wild ride north, south and then down the super-highway the trio noticed it was only 8:32, on the Union Electric clock on Market, so they stopped for breakfast at the De Luxe. They knew that they couldn't get anything to eat downtown and lunch might be hard to get at Stix. So gulp it down at the De Luxe and away again in the car to park on Franklin and Seventh and just make Stix for its opening at 9 a.m.

So begins the long sit. But, this being a special day with tests going on in other stores, too, a couple of the boys go over to Neisner's, sit down, are refused service, still sit. The manager comes over, boiling and bubbling, threatening to throw them out, have them arrested, beaten up; and also to fire all his Negro employees. He'll do this if the boys aren't out in five minutes, but they hold his ear for thirty, and Walter Hayes finally calms him down, and he returns out to be a pretty decent guy. A full-dress conference is arranged for January, after the holiday rush, and the boys and the manager part friends, shaking hands all around.

Then it's back to Stix to sit. But now pictures are needed of the sitting boys and girls at Mc-Crory, Woolworth and Katz Drug Stores (Walgreen serves, so no tests there this Saturday). A camera is loaded with super-fast film, and we have pictures of all the places, with no trouble, except at the Katz store at Eighth and Washington, where the manager becomes threatening, but the picture has already been taken. That's the store where the manager tries to provoke the CORE people by stacking dishes full of garbage on the counter in front of them.

The last photographs are at Woolworth's at Washington and Broadway. Here there is a lily-white counter with plenty of empty seats and at the other end a jim crow stand-up bar in a dark corner. It's so dark it's hard to tell if the pictures will come out, but they ought to be seen by everybody in the community. Perhaps that would at least shame people away from that jim crow place. Can't something be done to make people so ashamed they'll never, never patronize such a place in St. Louis?

Now the boys are back again at Stix to sit out the rest of the long day. The store officials and detectives keep themselves busy buzzing the CORE members, counting them. About half the seats are taken up, CORE members sitting one apart so that the other customers have to sit between them, and they often talk to them, give them the special CORE holiday greeting circular. Many customers leave very friendly toward CORE, expressing sympathy with its aims.

At five the quitting whistle blows for CORE, and some go to a CORE party, others out home, for Billie and Mervene and Greg must get home, and lots of other people have families waiting for them, and that hot meal at home looks good after a whole day of just sitting and no eating. Hot food, hot bath, aching back from those backless stools at Stix, and still the evening to go through. Work, play, read, write, do everything that must still be done. So long a day, but on they go, Saturday's children, and they hope to see you next Saturday.

Dagen Wants Letters—And He's Willing To Pay

by Irvin Dagen

Have you ever been at sea, at night, and looked up to the stars for guidance? There is the seemingly solid sky (made up of countless particles of dust) and in it, shining brightly, are the stars.

So it is with mankind. One among many will shine. And not only for his own lifetime, but as a guiding light for years after his death. We had one such star in our country for forty years. He shone from his young manhood at the turn of the century until his tragic death in an auto accident in 1938. He was 67 years old when he died, but still shining so brightly it seemed a young man had passed away.

Think of his deeds: Poet, musician, novelist, diplomatic official, lawyer, teacher, organizer for the NAACP. Never a moment slipped by but he was thinking about a way out. Who was he? James Weldon Johnson, author of a dozen books, best known of which are "God's Trombones," "Along This Way" and "The Autobiography of an Ex-Colored Man."

If you read nothing else, I think this "Autobiography" will give you an education. When it was first published, in 1912, it did not bear the author's signature. And it was surprising to find how many people claimed to be its author. For at that time "passing" was a more popular pastime.

But there is much more, infinitely more than the problem of "passing" in this book. It is so wise a book that today, forty years after it was written, nobody has shown more understanding or better insight into what the race problem has done to both white America and dark America.

And always the question is with us: HOW CAN WE WIPE OUT JIM-CROW? How can we get over this bump in the road and get on to living as normal, decent, free Americans should be living?

Shall each race crawl into its private shell, admit defeat, and say that peace will come only by complete, final, permanent segregation?

Shall we state flatly that only total, unequivocal and immediate interracialism will answer our needs?

Shall one race always keep in the background, begging for favors, jumping with joy for even the smallest of these favors?

And is it possible in St. Louis to say: I WILL NEVER KNOWINGLY PATRONIZE A JIM-CROW PLACE? Can we live in St. Louis and really do this? With the schools, the churches, the hotels, the restaurants and the hundred large and small social taboos? I say: IT CAN'T BE DONE! (and that holds for Negro and white).

But I also put this challenge: ARE WE DOING ENOUGH TO BREAK DOWN JIM-CROW? I know there are today enough places in downtown St. Louis serving on an interracial basis, so that there is no good excuse for eating jim-crow. There are printed lists of these places you can get by writing for one to this column.

And there are still other places, not on the list, and which I can't disclose as yet, which WILL serve you if you come in and sit down and ask for service as you ask for it in any other department. And here's another challenge: Next time you are downtown, drop into a restaurant, or a cafeteria, or a department store or a dime store. Go to the eating counter. AND I DON'T MEAN THE JIM-CROW COUNTER. It may surprise you to find how many places WILL serve.

You may be turned down. But you will have shown these people who run the restaurant or the store that THEY LIE WHEN THEY SAY YOU DON'T WANT TO EAT THERE. They say you like jim-crow. I've talked to dozens of them and always they throw this up to me. I DON'T BELIEVE IT. In hundreds of interracial tests we have shown them. But they need thousands of tests, and there are the numbers to make them.

There are, according to some late census figures, about 20 per cent Negroes in the St. Louis population. I believe that's the largest Negro population in any city where Negroes are allowed to vote freely. There's a bill up before the Board of Aldermen, introduced by Alderman Redmond, which would make it illegal to discriminate in eating places. HOW IS THAT 20 PER CENT OF THE VOTE GOING TO MAKE ITSELF HEARD SO THAT THIS BILL IS PASSED?

I want answers, and I'm willing to pay for them. For every letter I get from a reader, with good answers to some of the questions I've raised in this column, I'll send you a free book. Not any book, but one of my favorite books: JAMES WELDON JOHNSON'S "AUTOBIOGRAPHY OF AN EX-COLORED MAN."

In that way I will learn from you, and you will learn from the book. Is that a fair exchange? I think so. So let's hear from you.

faced the disappointment of watching opened doors swing closed again. Such was the situation at Chippewa Drug Stores. In August 1952, *Up to Date with CORE* reported:

> Since the change in policy . . . about two years ago, we have usually received good service. About two months ago, however, there was a sudden lapse of good service at the Grand and St. Louis Chippewa store. Steve Best talked with the store manager's superior, Mr. Weidner. Good service was restored and lasted for about two weeks.
>
> During the last two weeks, the following incidents have occurred at the Grand and St. Louis store. Several colored people were told they could not eat in the store but could take food out. The store manager said he didn't want Negro business, but that they would be served in their turn.
>
> Franso Griffin and Howard Harris sat at a table and were told it was reserved. They moved to the counter where they were asked what they wanted to take out. When they refused the take-out offer, the waitress said she was too busy to wait on them.
>
> Walter Hayes refused an offer to take something out and was finally served a malted milk in a large jelly glass.
>
> Franso refused a sack handed to him by a waiter after Franso asked for a cheeseburger to eat at the counter. Since the waiter hurriedly grabbed something from under the counter without taking time to put anything on the grill, we are inclined to think there was something other than a cheeseburger in the sack.

On July 14, Willis Lomax and John Woodson waited two hours after they were told they would be served when the waitresses had time. CORE recounted the incidents in a letter to Weidner, secretary of the company, and when

Steve Best telephoned a few days later, Weidner agreed with CORE that "those actions were direct violations of company policy."

He must have communicated that to the local staff because several customers were given prompt and courteous treatment as a result. Nevertheless, CORE members promised to frequently test the store. Giving up was not part of their plan.

Six

Other Confrontations

CORE did not limit its demonstrations to dime stores and drugstores or, for that matter, to eating facilities. Walter Hayes wrote of a project that reflected the diversity of CORE activities:

> This occurred in the early 1950s. St. Louis city operated a beautiful swimming pool, located in Fairgrounds Park. Blacks were not permitted to swim in this pool. We chose it as one of our projects because taxes paid by black citizens helped to pay for this pool.
>
> The day that CORE members decided to swim there I remember only three of us—Joe Ames, Marvin Rich and myself. We had no problem getting into the pool. However, word spread quickly around the neighborhood. Hundreds of white residents crowded around the pool fence to vent their feelings and to display their hatred.
>
> This memory stands out in my mind because, before this incident, I never knew that hatred actually traveled in waves. I could feel and see those hate waves, similar to heat waves coming at you on a hot, sunny day in a desert, coming from the crowd. It was an eerie feeling. We remained in the pool for about an hour and then left, without any violent incident. Shortly thereafter, the pool was filled in and tennis courts now exist where the pool was.

Marvin Rich also remembered that day:

> There was this mob outside. They didn't bother me too much. They would curse, but cops were holding

them back. But we were swimming and the life-
guards would spit at me.

My problem was, I was a lousy swimmer, and I
was scared that a lifeguard would swim by me and
grab my arm, and I would go under, and I would
never come up. What pulled me through was the
CORE sense of discipline, that I HAD to do it. It was
Walter and me, together.

One of the most popular cafeterias in St. Louis during
the 1950s was the Forum, located on Seventh Street just
west of Famous-Barr. It became the site of serious con-
frontations between CORE and the Christian Nationalists,
the national organization headed by Gerald L. K. Smith.
Joe Ames recalled several incidents:

> We would put several people inside with a black
> member at the head of the line and when that per-
> son was refused service, the other members, mostly
> white, would stay in line and refuse to go around.
> Meanwhile, one or more people would remain out-
> side, passing out leaflets to ingoing customers ex-
> plaining why the service was so slow and urging
> them to ask the management to serve everyone.
>
> About the second time we went there, an older
> man, a member of the Christian Nationalists, used
> an unnecessary amount of muscle in pushing past
> the lineup outside. The manager calmed him down.
> On another occasion, I was outside distributing
> leaflets and was verbally abused and then kicked by
> another of Smith's main functionaries.
>
> Marvin Rich was hit from the rear with a rolled-
> up magazine as he boarded a street car after the
> demonstration ended.
>
> On another day, I was assaulted by another of
> Smith's muscle men who shoved me up against the
> building, wrenched the stack of leaflets out of my
> hand, and then jumped into a car. Both he and I were

arrested. Mark Hennelly represented me, without fee, and I was found not guilty of anything. My assailant was found guilty and fined.

· Doris Marglous Nugent remembered another conflict with Smith's supporters, which took place during a CORE protest march at Kiel Auditorium on the night of a Smith rally:

> As we marched along the sidewalk with our anti-fascist signs held high, Smith's supporters passed between and around us, and there were angry verbal exchanges.
>
> Suddenly the St. Louis police grabbed some of our people and hoisted and pushed them across the sidewalk and into police cars. They manhandled our peaceable marchers, shoving them as forcefully and roughly as they could. Our marchers were non-violent and law-abiding. They were opposing wrong, yet doing it civilly. It was a sudden view into the maw of evil, that made the great need and pain of the struggle against racism and abusive power come alive.

Bonnie Marglous Rosen recalled many sit-ins at the Greyhound Bus Station, Stix, Baer & Fuller, and Pope's Cafeteria:

> I also remember picketing the American Theater on a very cold and windy night when Eva LeGallienne and Joseph Schildkraut were appearing in *The Cherry Orchard*. I had been invited to see the play and had to refuse. As we circled around, clutching our signs, I felt a twinge of regret. Couldn't I have compromised just this once? But on that wintry night, we were warmed with success when a group of delegates to an International Ladies Garment Workers Union convention refused to cross our picket line.

Although the activity (or inactivity) of sitting-in was essentially boring, we shared a spirit of adventure, had fun among ourselves, and laughed together at the absurdity of segregation. We passed the time chatting or reading, sometimes studying, sitting for several hours, while nothing happened. Or so it seemed.

Actually, something was happening. We were not verbally or physically abused; we were simply shunned. Waitresses gave us a wide berth, pretending not to see us; and people at other tables avoided looking at us. Certainly there was disapproval in that shunning. I think people also felt queasy, embarrassed to be eating, while we were refused service. We were shaking up the status quo, and they didn't know how to behave. So they pretended we were not there. But we did not go away.

Our training had prepared us to respond to taunts, insults or threats of violence in a nonviolent manner. I remember being warned to carefully inspect any food that might be served us, should there be slivers of glass, crushed cigarettes or cockroaches mixed in. It never happened.

But Charles Oldham recalled that something like that may have happened when two CORE members tested a store near the corner of Grand and Olive:

They were served, but somebody apparently put something [in] their food and within a half-hour both of them got deathly sick. We went back and filed a formal complaint, and they were very, very apologetic. Apparently, something had been done by one of their employees, and we didn't have any trouble after that. They were concerned about someone filing a lawsuit. That was the farthest thing from our minds. Nobody was going to make a claim. This was something we anticipated might happen.

CORE members were not surprised or discouraged by such potential threats to their well-being. They met taunts and malice in many places, and they never knew whether they would be welcomed (and if so, usually reluctantly) or openly ostracized when they sat down at lunch counters or tables. The July 1951 issue of *Up to Date with CORE* mentions that one team had already tested Shopper's Lunch, a small downtown restaurant, and relates the reception the second team received when they followed up:

> A week later, Rose Parnas and Marian O'Fallon were served. Joe Ames observed both these tests. After Rose and Marian were served, Joe heard the manager say that they should have put poison in the sandwiches.
>
> One of the waitresses scolded the waiter who served the CORE members.

Perhaps the most significant attributes of those early CORE members were their extraordinary patience and their staunch determination not to show anger at uncivil treatment. Sometimes they were sorely tested.

One night in 1949, Rose Parnas and Wanda Penny sat at Teutenberg's downtown restaurant from six until after midnight, waiting to be served. Two years before she died, Rose recalled the incident:

> Wanda and I went in there for dinner. I was asked what I would like, and I said Wanda could order first, and I would look at the menu. There was some staring, someone got on the phone, and they didn't give us any more attention. And so we sat. It got later and later.
>
> Near midnight they said they were closing and we could leave now. We said we wouldn't leave until we ate. Wanda said, "You do what you need to do, and we'll do what we need to do."

They called the police, who came in and said, "You know you have to leave. The restaurant is closing." We said we had come to open food accommodations to everyone, and so we wouldn't leave until we ate. One of them got mad and said, "Would you like to have a meal in jail?" I asked if I could make one phone call to my lawyer (I didn't have a lawyer) and said, "Do you want this to hit the newspapers? That you're dragging off two women who came to eat?"

Rose admitted that at this point she began to get mad, but Wanda came over and sat by her as the confrontation continued:

The officers looked at each other and looked at the manager and said, "What can we do?" The manager said, "Carry 'em out." And [one] officer said, "Why in hell don't you just give them a sandwich?"

So we got a sandwich. They brought mine, and I gave it to Wanda. Then they brought another one. After we ate, they said, "It's on the house." We said, "No way." They sold it to us, and we paid for it. We said we were sorry they didn't have enough help to serve us until 1 o'clock in the morning.

When recalling Wanda Penny and the other CORE members who regularly faced such hostility, Irv Dagen said,

I think what should be said about Wanda, the other people as well, was that they were willing to sacrifice, for they did not know if there would be retribution. She just went about her business, and that was a real inspiration to a great many people. Many were unwilling to come forward, unwilling to make the statement that something ought to be changed.

Maggie Dagen said, "Many people believed in what we were doing, but told us they could not do it. They were fearful they could not remain nonviolent. They did not have the patience required."

Vera Williams Rhiney valued her experiences with CORE. When she and a friend, Alice Parham, were refused service at the Famous-Barr lunch counter after shopping in the store all day, they went to talk to the manager. He asked them if they were with CORE. They had never heard of the organization, but they decided to find out about it, and they both joined CORE the next week.

Al Park remembered that he might have lost his job, but for the understanding of his boss:

> My boss, a vice president of Bemis Bag Company, received a phone call from a man who, as I remember, was executive secretary of the St. Louis Restaurant Association. He asked my boss if he knew what I was doing with CORE and if he realized that if my employment with Bemis were to be publicized, it would be detrimental to the company. My boss's response was that what I did on my own time was my business and he didn't appreciate the threat of negative publicity.
>
> I always loved that man!

In 1949, Jane Gaz, a student in the George Warren Brown School of Social Work at Washington University, participated in sit-ins at Stix, Baer & Fuller. Dean Benjamin Youngdahl called her into his office one day and said he had received an anonymous letter. The writer, having seen Jane seated at a counter with an interracial group he described as "Communist Agitators," had demanded that she be dismissed from the school. Youngdahl tore the letter into shreds and threw it into the wastebasket, assuring Jane that he fully supported her.

These often anonymous letters, sent by the opposition, were as much a test of the CORE members' patience and goodwill as were the uncivil attitudes of many restaurant owners. Billie Ames Teneau remembered that the National Citizens Protective Association was a leading opposition group. Their newsletter was called the *White Sentinel:*

> This publication often contained wildly incorrect and negative information about CORE. . . . Pamphlets were distributed urging white people to attend the regular meetings of the White Sentinel group.
>
> The Christian Nationalist Party also distributed a pamphlet headed, "White Man, Awaken!" This literature denounced "mongrelizers" and pointed toward segregation as "God's plan."
>
> My most direct contact with such opposition to integration came one Sunday morning as my two children and I emerged from the front door of our home, on our way to the Ethical Society Sunday School. There on our front lawn were the charred remains of a burned cross.
>
> I went inside, told my husband, then proceeded with my children to Sunday School. He informed the police. That afternoon a couple of policemen visited us and asked if we had any idea why the cross had been burned on our lawn and asked if we had ever had any trouble with our neighbors. We told them there had not been any trouble with neighbors and that the cross may have resulted from our sometimes having Negro guests.
>
> The policemen recommended that we not have any more Negro guests and said there had been several anti-Negro incidents in that area recently.
>
> No change was made in the persons invited to our home.

Seven

One Door Opens; Others Remain Closed

Enactment of the public accommodations ordinance in 1961 marked a hard-won victory for social justice in St. Louis. Irv Dagen expressed the view of early CORE members when he said, "We feel that CORE deserves much credit for the spade work that ultimately resulted in passage of the ordinance."

The battle, to be sure, had not been CORE's alone. But the demonstrators' patience and persistence had won the support of many church and community groups. At city hall, a minority of the board of aldermen had been pushing for legal enforcement of equality in public accommodations for thirteen years.

Three of the twenty-eight St. Louis aldermen, Jasper C. Caston, Walter Lowe, and Sidney R. Redmond, had first introduced the legislation on May 6, 1948. Their bill, Board Bill No. 62, read, in part:

> All persons within the City of St. Louis shall be entitled, without discrimination or segregation, to the full accommodations, advantages and facilities, and the privileges, of any place of public accommodations. . . . It shall be unlawful for any persons being the owner, lessee, proprietor, manager, superintendent, agent, servant, or employee of any such place, directly or indirectly, to exclude, discriminate against, refuse, withhold from or deny to, any person any of the accommodations, advantages, facilities or privileges thereof. . . .

At the time the legislation was first introduced, in a fortuitous coincidence, the Freedom Train, carrying the Declaration of Independence, other historic documents, and a replica of the Liberty Bell, stopped in St. Louis on its cross-country tour. Always looking for ways to press its campaign, CORE distributed leaflets to the members of the public visiting the Freedom Train. The leaflets contained the text of the proposed ordinance and a well-known quotation from the Declaration of Independence: "We hold these truths to be self-evident, that all men are created equal, that they are endowed by their Creator with certain unalienable Rights, that among these are Life, Liberty and the pursuit of Happiness." The leaflet urged people to support the aldermanic bill and to communicate their support to the aldermen.

The Freedom Train proved to be a popular exhibit and attracted large numbers of visitors. The exhibit was particularly relevant, following, as it did, close on the heels of World War II. The documents in the exhibit proclaimed the democratic ideals that had inspired the Allied war effort. However, the lofty goals America had fought for were not always expressed in domestic policies. This was 1948, and St. Louis, along with much of the country, remained mired in segregation and discrimination.

As CORE passed out leaflets urging passage of the public accommodations bill, Christian Nationalists, calling themselves the Racial Purity Committee, circulated an initiative petition for a law to enforce a "Separation of the Races." Their petition stated, "It shall be unlawful for any member of one race to use or occupy, any entrance, exit or seating or standing section set aside and assigned to the use of the other race."

For lack of support, their petition quickly died. It did

Board Bill No. 62
Introduced May 6, 1948
Messrs. Caston, Lowe, and Redmond
by request

BOARD BILL No. 62

AN ORDINANCE relating to the prevention and elimination, in the use of places and accommodations open to the public, of practices of discrimination and segregation, because of religion, race, creed, color, or national origin, making such practices unlawful, providing penalties for violation of the ordinance, and containing an emergency clause.

BE IT ORDAINED BY THE CITY OF ST. LOUIS, AS FOLLOWS:

Section 1. This ordinance shall be known as the Civil Rights Ordinance of the City of St. Louis. It shall be deemed as intended to promote the general welfare of all the people of the City of St. Louis and to secure to all persons the right of life, liberty, the pursuit of happiness and the enjoyment of the gains of their own industry, and the equal rights and opportunities under the law to which they are entitled by virtue of the provisions of Article I, Section 2 of the Bill of Rights of the Constitution of Missouri.

Section 2. The Board of Aldermen of the City of St. Louis declares that the practices of exclusion, segregation and discrimination in the use, operation and enjoyment of public places and accommodations against any of the residents of the city, or of those coming within its boundaries, because of race, religion, creed, color, or national origin, are in derogation of fundamental civil rights of the individuals, and also threaten the principal office of free democratic government.

Section 3. All persons within the City of St. Louis shall be entitled, without discrimination or segregation, to the full accommodations, advantages and facilities, and the privileges, of any place of public accommodations, resort, amusement or entertainment, subject only to the conditions, restrictions and limitations prescribed or established by law and applicable alike to all persons indiscriminately. It shall be unlawful for any persons being the owner, lessee, proprietor, manager, superintendent, agent, servant, or employee of any such place, directly or indirectly, to exclude, discriminate against, refuse, withhold from or deny to, any person any of the accommodations, advantages, facilities or privileges thereof, or to directly or indirectly publish, circulate, distribute, issue, display, print or mail any written or printed communication, notice, sign or advertisement to the effect that any of the accommodations, advantages, facilities, or privileges of any such place is, or shall be, refused, withheld from, curtailed, or denied to any person on account of religion, race, creed, color, or national origin, or that the patronage or custom thereat of any person belonging or purporting to be of any particular religion, race, creed, color, or national origin, is excluded, segregated, unwelcome, objectionable, or not acceptable, undesired or not solicited, and any person who shall violate or fail to comply with any of the provisions of this ordinance shall be deemed guilty of a misdemeanor, and, upon conviction thereof, shall be punished by a fine of not less than Twenty-Five Dollars ($25.00) nor more than Five Hundred Dollars ($500.00).

Section 4. A place of public accommodations. resort, amusement or entertainment, within the meaning of this ordinance, shall be deemed to include, but not be restricted to: inns, hotels, cafeterias, lunch rooms, roadhouses, auto courts and rooming houses whether operated and conducted for the entertainment of transient guests or for the accommodation of those seeking health, recreation, or rest or lodging, and restaurants or eating houses, or any place where food or drink is sold for consumption on the premises, stores, parks, or enclosures, confectioneries, soda fountains, and all stores where ice cream, ice and fruit preparations or their derivatives, are sold for consumption on the premises, drug stores, dispensaries, clinics, hospitals, bathhouses, theatres, motion picture houses, auditoriums, airdomes, roof gardens, music halls, race courses skating rinks, amusement and recreation halls and parks, fairs, bowling alleys, gymnasiums, shooting galleries, billiard and pool parlors, public libraries, museums, garages, public conveyances of all kinds and types whether operated on land or water or in the air, as well as stations and terminals for such conveyances.

Section 5. Nothing in this ordinance contained shall be construed to include that part of any private institution, club, lodge or organization which is (1) limited to persons holding an annual membership therein; (2) not engaged in soliciting memberships among the general public, and (3) nor dispensing services, accommodations, merchandise, food or liquids to non-members as a part of its regular endeavors.

Section 6. The passage of this ordinance being deemed necessary for the immediate preservation of the public health and safety, an emergency is hereby declared to exist and this ordinance shall take effect immediately upon its approval by the Mayor.

Flyer prepared by St. Louis CORE for distribution to visitors to the Freedom Train, St. Louis, May 1948: (front) St. Louis Board of Aldermen Bill No. 62

Wasn't the FREEDOM TRAIN a great experience?

Now, do you want to do something to make that LIBERTY BELL ring out? Take this home, and read it:

The DECLARATION OF INDEPENDENCE SAYS:

"We hold these truths to be self-evident, that all men are created equal, that they are endowed by their Creator with certain inalienable Rights, that among these are Life, Liberty and the pursuit of Happiness."

The St. Louis Board of Aldermen has before it a bill to ratify the DECLARATION OF INDEPENDENCE for the citizens of St. Louis.

Won't you please write to:

MR. HERMAN NOVACK
Chairman, Legislative Committee
Board of Aldermen, City Hall
St. Louis, Missouri

Write to him and tell him that you are for this bill, Board Bill No. 62.

A copy of this bill is printed inside this folder. Additional copies may be secured free by writing to:

FATHER JACK WHITE St. Malachy's Church 2929 Clark	**REV. J. M. PETTIGREW** Lane Tabernacle Church 4371 Enright
RABBI FERDINAND M. ISSERMAN Temple Israel 5017 Washington	**MR. J. HUTTON HYND** Ethical Society 3646 Washington

REV. GEO. EASTER
Christ Church Episcopal Cathedral
1210 Locust

(back) message to those visiting the traveling exhibits of the Liberty Bell and the Declaration of Independence.

RACIAL PURITY COMMITTEE

INITIATIVE PETITION FOR CITY ORDINANCE FOR

SEPARATION OF THE RACES

To the Honorable Board of Election Commissioners of The City of St. Louis, Missouri:

We, the undersigned legal and registered voters of The City of St. Louis, Missouri, respectfully petition that under the provisions of Article V of the Charter of The City of St. Louis, Missouri, there be submitted to the legal voters of said City, to be voted upon as provided by said article of said Charter, the following ordinance, to-wit:

AN ORDINANCE

Regulating separation of the races, and providing a penalty for its violation.

Be it ordained by The City of St. Louis, as follows:

Section One. It shall be unlawful for any person in charge or control of any room, hall, theatre, picture house, auditorium, yard, court, ball park, public park, or other indoor or outdoor place, to which both white persons and negroes are admitted, to cause, permit or allow therein or thereon any theatrical performance, picture exhibition, speech, or educational or entertainment program of any kind whatsoever, unless such room, hall, theatre, picture house, auditorium, yard, court, ball park, or other place, has entrances, exits and seating or standing sections set aside for and assigned to the use of white persons, and other entrances, exits and seating or standing sections set aside for and assigned to the use of negroes, and unless the entrances, exits and seating or standing sections set aside for and assigned to the use of white persons are distinctly separated from those set aside for and assigned to the use of negroes, by well defined physical barriers, and unless the members of each race are effectively restricted and confined to the sections set aside for and assigned to the use of such race.

Section Two. It shall be unlawful for any member of one race to use or occupy any entrance, exit or seating or standing section set aside for and assigned to the use of members of the other race.

Section Three. It shall be unlawful for any person to conduct, participate in or engage in any theatrical performance, picture exhibition, speech, or educational or entertainment program of any kind whatsoever, in any room, hall, theatre, picture house, auditorium, yard, court, ball park, public park, or other indoor or outdoor place, knowing that any provision of the two preceding sections has not been complied with.

Section Four. The Chief of Police and members of the Police Department shall have the right, and it shall be their duty, to disperse any gathering or assemblage in violation of this ordinance, and to arrest any person guilty of violating the same.

Section Five. Any violation of this ordinance shall be punishable by fine of up to five hundred dollars or imprisonment up to ninety days or both.

Section Six. If any provision of this ordinance or the application of any provision to any person or circumstances shall be held invalid, the validity of the remainder of the ordinance and the applicability of such provision to other persons or circumstances shall not be affected thereby.

And we hereby designate by name and residence address the following five persons as the committee of the petitioners, as provided by law, to-wit:

Opal M. Tanner, 3204 Hawthorne Blvd. (8)   John W. Hamilton, 3965 Westminster, (17)   Hermine A. Beck, 3615 Shenandoah Ave. (15)
Don Lohbeck, 1533 S. Grand Ave. (16)   Joseph F. Intagliata, 8116 Vulcan St. (11)

all in the City of St. Louis, Missouri.

And each of the undersigned for himself says: I am a resident and a legal and registered voter of The City of St. Louis, Missouri; I have personally signed this petition and I have correctly written after my name my residence address in said City.

Do not fill Ward Pct.		NAME	RESIDENCE ADDRESS (Give House Number and Street)	DO NOT FILL
		1.		
		2.		
		3.		
		4.		
		5.		
		6.		
		7.		
		8.		
		9.		
		10.		
		11.		
		12.		
		13.		
		14.		
		15.		
		16.		
		17.		
		18.		
		19.		
		20.		

STATE OF MISSOURI } ss.
CITY OF ST. LOUIS

The below subscribed Affiant, being duly sworn, on his oath says that each of the above signatures to the foregoing petition was made in Affiant's presence by, as Affiant verily believes, the person whose name it purports to be.

_____
(Signature of Affiant)

Subscribed and sworn to before me this_____ day of_____, 194 .

My term expires_____   _____ Notary Public.

(When filled return to Racial Purity Committee, 1533 S. Grand Blvd., St. Louis.)

Petition circulated by the Christian Nationalists when the public accommodations bill was before the St. Louis Board of Aldermen in 1948. See appendix 2 for full text.

not gain enough signatures for a public vote. But at the same time, the St. Louis Board of Aldermen was not yet ready to grant African Americans free access to public eating establishments, hotels, bowling alleys, and theaters. The 1948 bill was rejected.

CORE members took the failure as a challenge and redoubled their efforts to bring about change through negotiation and nonviolent direct action, even as the Christian Nationalists harassed them and threatened violence. CORE members saw that the social climate and the public's views were changing. Some St. Louisans agreed with CORE's philosophy but thought its members were ahead of their time, caught up in a wave of idealistic enthusiasm. Gradually, more and more community groups endorsed opening public accommodations to all, and CORE's campaign for legislation gathered strength.

The climate was changing, too, at city hall. In December 1954, as community support for CORE's efforts grew, a second public accommodations bill was introduced by the board of aldermen. As noted in *Up to Date with CORE* in January 1955, CORE members called meetings with a number of community leaders to insure interracial and bipartisan sponsorship and endorsement of the bill. The St. Louis Council on Human Relations had won inclusion of all public accommodations in the proposed legislation as well as a provision setting up a conciliation agency to attempt settlement of complaints before initiation of any court action.

Among the groups supporting the bill were the Metropolitan Church Federation, the National Council of Jewish Women, the Catholic Commission on Race Discrimination, the Urban League, and the NAACP. But even the combined pressure exerted by these organizations could not overcome aldermanic opposition. Once more, the St.

Louis Board of Aldermen defeated the public accommo-
dations bill, this time by a vote of seventeen to ten. The
aldermen who voted for ending discrimination in 1954
were Democrats William Brady, John T. Curry, Edgar J.
Freely, William K. Gardner, Alfred I. Harris, De Witte T.
Lawson, James W. Noonan, and Clinton J. Watson and
Republicans William A. Stolar and Sidney Redmond.
Voting against the legislation were Democrats Louis
Aboussie, who represented the Eastern Europeans and
Lebanese in the Soulard neighborhood; Louis G. Berra,
who represented the Italians on the Hill, the biggest ward
in the city; A. J. Cervantes, who represented a middle-
class ward in the center of the city; Carl Gassel, a German
from north St. Louis; Raymond Leisure, who represented
Lebanese in the La Salle Park area; Albert Villa, who rep-
resented Italian and German Catholic factory workers in
the south St. Louis neighborhood of Carondelet; Leo J.
McLaughlin, who represented the Irish in the northern-
most ward of the city; A. Barney Mueller, a north-side
German; Anton Niemeyer, a south-side German; Joseph
Roddy, an Irishman from the near south side by Forest
Park; and Everett Taylor. Republicans George J. Grellner,
Carl Guetschow, Fred Haag, Melvin E. Krah, and Ray
Lohse, all from predominantly German neighborhoods,
and board president Charles E. Albanese, an Italian, also
voted against the bill.

St. Louis in the 1950s was an ethnic patchwork. The
north side of the city was made up of Irish Catholics and
German Protestants. Near the river on the north side lived
poor whites who had come from the Ozarks during the
war to work in the defense industries. In the central cor-
ridor, west of downtown's skyscrapers, African Americans lived in Mill Creek Valley between the factories that
lined the railroad tracks. Wealthy families lived in the

Central West End near Forest Park and also to the south in Compton Heights near Tower Grove Park. Black professionals lived in the Ville, just north of the Central West End, and the student population at Soldan High School north of Forest Park was predominantly Jewish. Directly south of Forest Park was the heavily Irish Dog Town. South from Dog Town lay the Hill, the Italian neighborhood, which had the largest population of any political ward in the country. South of downtown, in the Soulard neighborhood around the breweries, lived immigrants from Eastern Europe and Lebanon. The remaining wards of south St. Louis were made up of middle-class German Protestants and Catholics.

In the late 1950s the Mill Creek Valley land-clearance project displaced a large number of African Americans. Those families moved north and west, replacing the Irish, German, and Jewish families that moved west and north into St. Louis County. African Americans were able to elect new aldermen to represent them, and the public accommodations bill was brought up again. One version of the bill had died in committee in 1953, and a similar bill had died in committee in 1955. Public accommodations bills made it to the floor in 1956, 1958, 1959, and in the spring session of 1960, but they were all defeated. Yet another version of the bill died in committee in the fall session of 1960.

Disappointed but undeterred, members of CORE and others continued to work toward the passage of a public accommodations ordinance. Finally, thirteen years after the first bill was introduced, they reached their goal. In May 1961, eleven members of the St. Louis Board of Aldermen sponsored Ordinance No. 50553. On May 19, 1961, the ordinance passed by a vote of twenty to four, and it was enacted into law on June 1, 1961. It stated, in part:

Ordinance 50553
(B.B. No. 18)

This bill is introduced and sponsored by the following Members of the Board of Aldermen: Archie Blaine, A. J. Cervantes, William Clay, John T. Curry, Harold I. Elbert, John D. Gumersell, Al Harris, D. T. Lawson, T. H. Mayberry, Wayman F. Smith and Lawrence E. Woodson.

An ordinance defining discriminatory practices in places of public accommodation; prohibiting the same; and providing penalties for the violation thereof.

WHEREAS, each member of the Board of Aldermen recognizes that the government of the City of St. Louis was organized to protect and promote the health, safety, and welfare of all the residents of the City of St. Louis, including minority groups; and

WHEREAS, each alderman was elected by and is under a duty to represent all groups and segments of his constituency regardless of their race, color, creed, national ancestry, or origin; and

WHEREAS, each alderman is cognizant of his duty to protect and foster the welfare of persons residing in his ward and to prevent, insofar as possible, any discrimination in places of public accommodation regardless of a person's religious beliefs, and to insure that such person if he be a Catholic, Jew, Protestant, or a member of another religious sect, not be discriminated against in places of public accommodation; and

WHEREAS, each alderman is cognizant of his duty to protect and foster the welfare of persons residing in his ward and to prevent, insofar as possible, any discrimination in places of public accommodation regardless of a person's race, and to insure that such person if he be a Caucasian, Negro, or Mongolian, not be discriminated against in places of public accommodations; and

WHEREAS, each alderman is cognizant of his duty to protect and foster the welfare of persons residing in his ward and to prevent, insofar as possible, any discrimination in places of public accommodation regardless of a person's ancestry or national origin, and to insure that such person if he be English, Irish, French, Italian, Spanish, German, Hungarian, Austrian, Slav, Czech, Greek, Lithuanian, Armenian, Russian, Norwegian, Swedish, Polish, Syrian, African, Indian, Chinese, Japanese, Filipino, etc., not be discriminated against in places of public accommodations; and

WHEREAS, in order to insure that there be no discriminatory practices in places of public accommodations on account of race, color, religious beliefs, ancestry, or national origin, the Board of Aldermen, in order to protect the public welfare, hereby enact this ordinance. NOW, THEREFORE,

Be it ordained by the City of St. Louis, as follows:

Section One. It is hereby declared to be the policy of the City of St. Louis in the exercise of its licensing and police powers for the preservation of the peace and the protection of the comfort, health, welfare and safety of the City of St. Louis and the inhabitants thereof, to prohibit discriminatory practices in places of public accommodations as hereinafter defined.

Section Two. Definitions. When used herein:

(a) The term "person" includes one or more individuals, partnerships, associations, corporations, legal representatives, or other group of persons.

(b) The term "Council" means the St. Louis Council on Human Relations as defined in Ordinance No. 45184 of the ordinances of the City of St. Louis; and the term "Anti-Discrimination Division" means a special standing committee consisting of five (5) members of the St. Louis Council on Human Relations, said five members to be designated by the chairman of the St. Louis Council on Human Relations, each member so designated to be approved by a majority of the members of said Council.

(c) The phrase "places of public accommodation" means all places or businesses offering or holding out to

---

St. Louis Ordinance 50553 (the public accommodations ordinance), passed by the St. Louis Board of Aldermen on May 19, 1961, and enacted into law June 1, 1961.

the general public services or facilities for the peace, comfort, health, welfare and safety of such general public including, but not limited to, public places providing food, shelter, recreation and amusement.

Section Three. Discriminatory practices, as hereinafter defined and established, in places of public accommodation are hereby prohibited and declared unlawful.

(a) It shall be a discriminatory practice directly or indirectly to deny, refuse or withhold from any person, within the City of St. Louis, on account of race, color, religious beliefs, ancestry or national origin, full and equal accommodation advantages, facilities and privileges in all places of public accommodation.

(b) It shall be a discriminatory practice for the owner, lessee, manager, proprietor, concessionaire, custodian, agent or employee of a place of public accommodation within the City of St. Louis to treat differentially any person in such service or sale of privilege, facility, or commodity on account of race, color, religious beliefs, ancestry or national origin, or to segregate or require the placing of any person in any separate section or area of the premises or facilities, in such service or sale of privilege, facility or commodity, on account of race, color, religious beliefs, ancestry or national origin.

(c) It shall be a discriminatory practice to place, post, maintain, display, or circulate, or knowingly cause, permit or allow the placing, posting, maintenance, display or circulation of any written or printed advertisement, notice or sign of any kind or description to the effect that any of the accommodations, advantages, facilities or privileges of any place of public accommodation shall be refused, withheld from or denied to any person on account of race, color, religious beliefs, ancestry or national origin, or that the patronage of any person is unwelcome, objectionable, or not acceptable, desired or solicited on account of race, color, religious beliefs, ancestry or national origin, or that any person is required or requested to use any separate section or area of the premises or facilities on account of race, color, religious beliefs, ancestry, or national origin.

Section Four. The administration of this ordinance shall be the responsibility of the St. Louis Council on Human Relations. The Anti-Discrimination Division shall have full operating responsibility under the supervision of the Council for carrying out the provisions of this ordinance. In addition to any powers or duties heretofore conferred on said Council it shall have the power and duty to:

(a) Initiate on its own or receive, investigate and seek to adjust all complaints or discriminatory practices prohibited by this ordinance.

(b) By itself or through its Anti-Discrimination Division, to hold public or private hearings, subpoena witnesses and compel their attendance, administer oaths, take the testimony of any person under oath relating to any matter under investigation or in question. The Council may make rules as to the procedure for the issuance of subpoenas by the Anti-Discrimination Division. Contumacy or refusal to obey a subpoena issued pursuant to this section may be certified to a City Court of the City of St. Louis for appropriate action.

Section Five. Procedure.

(a) Any person claiming to be aggrieved by a discriminatory practice prohibited by this ordinance may make, sign and file with the St. Louis Council on Human Relations a complaint in writing under oath, which shall state the name and address of the person alleged to have committed the discriminatory practice and which shall set forth the particulars thereof and contain such other information as may be required by the Council. Such complaints shall be filed within thirty (30) days after the alleged discriminatory act is committed. The Council, at any time it has reason to believe that any person has been engaged in discriminatory practices prohibited by this ordinance, may issue a complaint.

(b) If the Anti-Discrimination Division determines after investigation that probable cause exists for the allegations made in the complaint, the Anti-Discrimination Division shall attempt an adjustment by means of conference and conciliation. Sixty (60) days shall be allowed for this purpose. If the Anti-Discrimination Division determines that there is no probable cause for the allegations made in the complaint, then they shall dismiss the complaint and promptly notify the complainant and the respondent of this action. If no action is taken by the Anti-Discrimination Division within ninety (90) days after the complaint is filed, such complaint shall hereby be considered dismissed.

(c) In case of failure of conference or conciliation to obtain compliance with this ordinance, the Anti-Discrimination Division may either certify the entire case to the City Counselor for prosecution, or cause to be issued and served in the name of the Council a written notice, together with a copy of such complaint, as the same may have been amended, requiring the person named in such complaint, hereinafter referred to as the respondent, to answer the charges of such complaint at a hearing before the Anti-Discrimination Division, at a time and place to be specified in such notice. The place of such hearing may be the office of the Council or another place designated by it. The case in support of the complaint shall be presented at the hearing by a member of the City Counselor's office who shall be counsel for the St. Louis Council on Human Relations; and no council member who previously made the investigation or caused the notice to be issued shall participate in the hearing except as a witness nor shall participate in the deliberations of the Anti-Discrimination Division in such case. Any endeavors or negotiations for conciliation or admission or statement made in connection therewith shall not be received in evidence. The respondent may file a written answer to the complainant and appear at such hearing in person or otherwise with or without counsel, and submit testimony and be fully heard. The Anti-Discrimination Division conducting any hearing may permit reasonable amendments to any complaint or answer and the testimony taken at such hearing

shall be under oath and be transcribed at the request of either party or by direction of the Anti-Discrimination Division. If, upon all the evidence, the Anti-Discrimination Division finds that a respondent has engaged in any discriminatory practice as defined in Section Three (3), it shall state its findings of fact and shall issue and file with the Council and cause to be served on the respondent an order requiring such respondent to cease and desist from such discriminatory practice or practices, or make such other order as the circumstances warrant. If, upon all the evidence, the Anti-Discrimination Division finds that the respondent has not engaged in any alleged discriminatory practice, it shall state its findings of fact and shall similarly issue and file an order dismissing the complaint. The Council shall establish rules of practices to govern, expedite and effectuate the foregoing procedure.

(d) If either the complainant or the respondent is not satisfied with the determination of the Anti-Discrimination Division, he shall have the right to appeal such discrimination to the Council within twenty (20) days after the date of such determination. No member of the Anti-Discrimination Division may participate in determination of an appeal. All decisions of the Council on such majority, a quorum, for determination of appeals, shall consist of six members. On appeal the Council may dismiss the complaint, affirm the Anti-Discrimination Divison's order or make such other appropriate order as shall effectuate the purposes of this ordinance.

(e) In the event the Anti-Discrimination Division shall have entered a cease and desist order from which no appeal is taken, and in those cases where such order is appealed and affirmed by the Council, the Council shall, in cases of noncompliance therewith, certify the entire case to the City Counselor for appropriate action. No prosecution shall be brought under this ordinance except upon such certification, provided, however, that in cases dismissed by failure of the Anti-Discrimination Division to act as provided in Section Five (b), or if the Anti-Discrimination Division dismisses a complaint, such dismissal being affirmed on appeal to the Council, the complainant may present such complaint directly to the City Counselor for such action as he shall deem advisable.

(f) All complaints, answers, investigations, conferences and hearings held under and pursuant to this ordinance shall be held confidential by the Council, the Anti-Discrimination Division and their agents and employees, provided, however, that the Anti-Discrimination Division may, at the request of the complainant, or on its own initiative, and shall, at the request of the respondent, declare the hearing provided for under Section Five (c) of this ordinance to be an open and public hearing.

(g) Within the limits of the listed specifications, the Anti-Discrimination Division shall have the power to formulate its own rules of procedure.

Section Six. Any persons violating any of the provisions of this ordinance shall be guilty of a misdemeanor and shall be fined not less than $25.00 nor more than $500.00.

Section Seven. If any of the provisions of this ordinance or portions thereof or the application of such provisions or portions to any person or circumstance shall be held invalid, the remainder of this ordinance and its application to persons or circumstances other than those to which it is held invalid shall not be affected thereby.

Section Eight. A copy of this ordinance shall be kept conspicuously posted in all places of public accommodation as herein defined and possessing any license from the City of St. Louis including such license for the conduct of business.

Approved: June 1, 1961.

> It is hereby declared to be the policy of the City of St.
> Louis in the exercise of its licensing and police pow-
> ers for the preservation of the peace and the protec-
> tion of comfort, health, welfare and safety of the City
> of St. Louis and the inhabitants thereof, to prohibit
> discriminatory practices in places of public accom-
> modations.

The eleven sponsors, black and white, were Archie
Blaine, A. J. Cervantes (who had opposed the previous
bill), William Clay, John T. Curry, Harold I. Elbert, John D.
Gummersell, Alfred I. Harris, D. T. Lawson, T. H. Mayberry, Wayman F. Smith, and Lawrence E. Woodson. Cervantes became mayor of St. Louis in 1965, and Clay was
elected to Congress in 1968. Other sponsors were well-
known lawyers and businessmen.

In the 1960s, the civil rights movement swept the country. Farmer's original plan for the interracial membership
of CORE to use Gandhian nonviolent, direct action to end
segregation gave way to "Black Power" and a growing
separation of the races.

Several members of St. Louis CORE became active in
CORE on the national level. Billie Ames became a paid
group coordinator of CORE in 1954, but she left that position in 1955. Henry Hodge, the black social worker who
had joined St. Louis CORE in 1947, helped to revitalize the
Los Angeles chapter of CORE in 1955 and became the national vice chairman of CORE in 1959. Charles Oldham, a
labor lawyer, served as the national chairman of CORE
from 1956 to 1963. Marvin Rich, an original member of St.
Louis CORE, joined the national action committee of
CORE in 1956 and was hired as the community relations
director in 1959.

Then in 1960 came the sit-in at the Woolworth's lunch
counter in Greensboro, North Carolina. As student civil

rights groups sprang up throughout the South, they turned to CORE for guidance. Oldham and other CORE leaders emphasized the original spirit and tactics of Gandhi. Oldham said, "We must widen and deepen the understanding of nonviolent direct action so that soul force, the Satyagraha of Gandhi, develops and transforms our society."

National CORE branched out to participate in Freedom Rides to integrate interstate buses and bus stations to participate in voter-registration drives in the South. In 1963 members of St. Louis CORE demonstrated at the Jefferson Bank to protest discrimination in employment, and the St. Louis media finally gave coverage to CORE. Some early members felt they could achieve the new goals and stayed active in CORE; others moved on to deal with racial and social issues through other venues. National CORE became the major civil rights organization at the center of the black protest movement, and as it did, the nature of the organization changed. The new members, young black activists, began to differentiate between integration and equality, and to choose the latter as their goal. The old methods and ideals of CORE were seldom brought up.

The original members of St. Louis CORE faced a period in which their interracial composition and Gandhian philosophy of patient negotiation and nonviolent direct action were challenged by hostile words and deeds. Originally St. Louis CORE had been formed as a "Committee OF Racial Equality." Members at that time practiced true personal equality in private and in public, in all their life activities, in their attitudes, and in their actions.

The small group no longer met at the Dagens' apartment or at the Centennial Christian Church. CORE members no longer sat neglected or poorly served at eating establishments. But the original members clung to their zeal for social justice for everyone, as they went forward in their varied endeavors. The convictions shared and the bonds forged in their struggle have remained strong in all the years since they began.

Eight

Winning Them Over

> The whole idea of CORE from the beginning, was to win over to our way of thinking people who initially were opposed to what we were trying to accomplish.
>
> —Irvin Dagen

Although originally limited to the tangible goal of equality in public accommodations, CORE had a larger purpose. Its goal of winning people over was based on the belief that change can occur in two ways (almost simultaneously): an outer change in practice requires an inner change of attitude but as practice and tradition change, so does attitude.

As doors opened, prejudice began to pale. New generations find it hard to realize that in 1947 restaurant doors were, figuratively speaking, locked against African Americans. Many St. Louisans who lived through those days of segregation and discrimination in public accommodations were unaware, at the time, of the eddies of change swirling around them. One of the purposes of this account is to recall how things were and how they have changed and to suggest how further changes may be made.

As noted earlier, CORE was begun in Chicago by theological students at the University of Chicago who adopted the Gandhian philosophy of nonviolence and direct action. They sought to bring about change through firm, persistent persuasion, focusing on the goal while always demonstrating goodwill. Their methods worked, not in a series of sudden, dramatic successes, but in a continuum of slow and steady progress over the years.

Bonnie Marglous Rosen described a positive outcome of CORE activities:

> Our mere presence was an excellent educational experience for the public. We were a living demonstration that young people of varying shades of skin color could be friends. Surely, many people, coming and eating and leaving while we sat unserved, noticed that we enjoyed each other's company and that we were peaceful and patient. I am certain that we gained a kind of respect, however puzzled or grudging.

CORE members did not appear defensive during demonstrations or stare angrily at the world. They were quietly at ease so that what might have initially shocked bystanders came to be seen as only natural. One of the greatest satisfactions CORE members experienced was to witness changes in attitude. Charles Oldham recalled:

> It was a remarkable experience to see the metamorphosis in individuals: managers, owners, employees, as you worked with them. It didn't happen overnight. It might take two or three years, but, at the end of the time, you became friendly and had an excellent relationship with people who started out really hating you.

Even at Stix, Baer & Fuller, where eighteen months of demonstrations did not yield a change in policy, Oldham remembered a change of heart:

> We sat there for eighteen months and we became friendly with the waitresses who wouldn't serve us and with the security people. They would talk to us

and discuss family and so on. I remember, after we left, we came back a year or two later, and they greeted us very happily. So we started out with an antagonistic audience at Stix, and we ended with a very friendly relationship, even though they didn't serve us. I think that was due, primarily, to the fact that we were non-violent, and we were courteous and well dressed, and we presented ourselves properly and never raised our voices.

CORE's long campaign at Pope's cafeteria made a convert of Harry Pope. Pope evolved from a stubborn resister to an advocate of equality. Irv Dagen described him:

He, and his father before him, ran a pretty substantial chain of cafeterias. It was no small operation. And they did some catering to factories and other places. And, of course, he was in the same position as all the others. He said, "My help won't like it; my customers won't like it."

I would say that the closest we ever came to a convert was Harry Pope. He was very influential. He was on the Mayor's Human Relations Commission. He was active in the Restaurant Association, and I think that a good deal of what happened all around was because of his influence. Maggie and I had contact with him for forty years.

But CORE's earliest negotiations with Harry Pope had been unsuccessful. In 1995, Maggie Dagen looked back on one fruitless meeting:

Wanda Penny and I went to Pope's Cafeteria near Grand Avenue on Washington, and he ushered us into his office, which was on the first floor. . . . He came up with the idea that we should send in somebody from CORE, starting with someone very light-skinned once a week, with a white person, and he would instruct his personnel to serve that person. The next week, a darker-skinned person would be sent in, and the following week an even darker-skinned individual. The idea was that personnel and customers would gradually accept a black. Wanda's face, I will never forget, was such a study, and I remember exactly what I said. I turned to him and said, "That's an interesting idea, Mr. Pope, but we are running a human relations organization, not a paint store."

When all the tests and negotiations had failed to change Harry Pope's mind, CORE began demonstrations at the cafeteria in May 1951. The May issue of *Up to Date with CORE* reported:

Near Violence at Pope's

On Saturday, May 12, seven CORE members stood in the Pope's Cafeteria line. A store employee stood in front of them so they could not move beyond the stack of trays. White customers moved around the CORE group. Charles Oldham went outside to instruct white CORE members who might be coming to the demonstration late. Charlie reentered with Bill Richards. They went around the CORE group, stopped in front of the meat counter and then identified themselves as CORE members.

The waitress told Mr. Pope, who turned to Charlie and said, "I want you to get out of here." Pope took Charlie's tray, and Charlie kept the silver. Then Pope came back, took the silver, held Charlie by the arm and shoved him. Charlie and Bill then moved to the end of the line of CORE members.

Outside, Charlie had reached Eleanor Smith by telephone and instructed her to come down and go around the CORE group, then identify herself with CORE. She did this and told the waitress that she planned to share her food with one of the colored

CORE members. Mr. Pope took her tray and said
that if she did not move, he would use force. After
he said it twice, Eleanor moved behind the other
CORE people. One employee hit Mary Washington
with his elbow and called her a "stupid thing." Mr.
Pope told the employee to be more careful. The employee was courteous after that.

More demonstrations were to come before Pope's Cafeteria opened to all, but in the course of the campaign, Harry Pope became a friend to his adversaries and a propo-
nent of civil rights. Charles Oldham recalled, "A couple of
years later, we were at some sort of discussion group, and
Harry was there. He was very friendly toward us. He had
kind thoughts about CORE and the people who were involved in it. I know that Irv had a lot to do with his conversion."

Maggie and Irv Dagen remembered that in later years,
whenever they saw Harry Pope, he would gleefully recall
Maggie's distinction between CORE and a paint store,
and that he always asked after Wanda Penny.

The success stories recounted here can only suggest the
level of sustained, painstaking effort that CORE members
invested in their campaigns. Even while they stayed in-
tensely focused on their work to eliminate racial discrimination in public accommodations, CORE members strove
constantly to widen their circle of support. From the first
appearance of *Up to Date with CORE,* in March 1951, every
issue contained reports of talks made by CORE members
to churches, clubs, schools, community organizations,
unions, and business and professional associations.

In 1952, two years before the Supreme Court ruling on
Brown v. the Board of Education struck down segregation in
public education, St. Louis CORE issued a plan to desegregate the St. Louis public schools. The Teamsters Union,

led by Harold Gibbons, printed and circulated the plan. Although the *St. Louis Post-Dispatch* had ignored CORE's campaign for equality in public accommodations, it now published an editorial urging adoption of the school-desegregation plan. The St. Louis public school administration rejected the plan out of hand, postponing action to desegregate the public schools until forced to do so.

No statistics are available to measure CORE's success in winning people over and easing the grip of prejudice in the community. But sweeping changes in policy, custom, and law suggest that CORE played an important role by effectively spreading its message and challenging more citizens to speak up for human justice. Early members of CORE became convinced of the power of nonviolent direct action.

Nine

In Their Own Words

A half century has passed since the founding of St. Louis CORE, but memories stay fresh in the minds of the men and women who, as young activists, sought to change the racial climate of their corner of the world. To document and preserve CORE's untold story, a small group of former members of St. Louis CORE got together in 1994 and distributed a questionnaire to other former participants. The questionnaire drew responses from thirty former members of CORE, some still in St. Louis and others living in New York, New Jersey, Washington, D.C., Maryland, Florida, California, and Alaska. What follows are their reminiscences, in their own words—memories of the early years, by those scattered members of St. Louis CORE.

In the summer of 1950, Steve Best came to St. Louis to join Cecil Hinshaw's Peace Army, a small group of people who visited church congregations to spread the doctrine of Gandhi. He remained in St. Louis and was employed by the Missouri Welfare Department:

> CORE's main appeal was the members' commitment to taking the necessary action to end segregation in a non-violent, Gandhian manner. At one time I was chairperson for approximately three months. That was a high point for me, because I had to increase my involvement and take on more important tasks. . . .
>
> I remember going to a restaurant on Franklin Avenue with Charlie Oldham to interview the owner. Charlie did the talking while I just stood there; the

tall, heavy, silent partner. The manager became quite
nervous and looked from one to the other of us. Finally, he blurted, "This is the heavy one, isn't he?"
Perhaps we reminded him of Mafia henchmen.

Steve and Joyce Best translated their CORE ideals into
a way of life, sharing a four-family flat in north St. Louis
with another white couple, a black couple, and an integrated couple. In 1995, Joyce Best wrote that her experiences in CORE provided her first participation in race relations:

> After teaching in the newly integrated St. Louis Pub-
> lic Schools, colleagues identified me as the white
> expert on black people, because they knew of my
> involvement in CORE. I later helped to form the
> Freedom of Residence group in St Louis.
> Those activities led to my participation in the
> Women's International League for Peace and Free-
> dom and in some national "undoing racism" work-
> shops.
> I believe that it takes longer today for some strate-
> gies to work. However, I am really encouraged to
> see the conflict-resolution approach being used in
> schools, communities and even in international set-
> tings.

Since her involvement in CORE, Joyce has been active in
other groups that promote peace and interracial harmony.
She enjoys membership in a dialogue group that includes
people of different races and backgrounds.

Eleanor Smith's interest in CORE was a natural out-
growth of her upbringing in a liberal home:

> My parents, followers of Eugene Debs and Norman
> Thomas, regarded racism as a major injustice. When
> I was eleven or so, my father took me to see the stage

production of Richard Wright's *Black Boy*. And one of my few memories of my mother, who died when I was quite young, is of her telling me, with feeling, about Gandhi in South Africa and then in India.

Of the sit-ins at lunch counters and the meetings, two things stand out: Joe Ames' laughter when a hostile person hit him with a length of pipe and hit his trousered, artificial leg; and my admiration for the courage and poise of the persons who talked reasonably, courteously, but perseveringly to managers.

Norman Winkler, too, grew up in an atmosphere where prejudice had no place:

I can't remember a single situation when my parents or I approved of discrimination. When I was growing up in south St. Louis, I puzzled over the fact that there were no Negro children in my school. My school, Woodward, was a new, modern brick building, while Negro children in the neighborhood attended old schools downtown or temporary "portable" schools.

I attended fascinating meetings at the Dagens' apartment. There were very interesting speakers and discussions on social, economic and political issues. I heard Bernice Fisher speak of CORE and its pacifist philosophy. I found it difficult to believe that passive resistance could be as powerful as she claimed. We did have the example of Gandhi, but that was India. However, I could see that it might work here as a strategy.

Henry Hodge was introduced to CORE by Joe Ames, whom he met at the Ethical Society:

My activity in St Louis CORE opened a world beyond Ewing and Washington, outside the ghetto. It served to point me in a positive direction, where I

could relate to different people. I met the giants of
CORE and nonviolent action: Wally and Juanita Nelson, Jim Farmer, Bayard Rustin, George Houser.
Meeting and talking with them made a lasting im-
pression on me. I was a youngster who was looking
for direction and a sense of purpose.

When Mary McClain McAllister learned she had been
accepted to graduate school at Washington University's
George Warren Brown School of Social Work, she prepared herself for life in a segregated city:

At first I was pleasantly surprised to find that I could
sit any place on the bus or streetcars. But I was un-
happy when the YWCA in downtown St. Louis referred me to the Phyllis Wheatley branch on Locust
Street which was reserved for women of African de-
scent.

Despite our heavy school assignments and field
placements, we made time to work for city-wide integration. I remember a day we spent at the downtown Woolworth lunch counter. I had my knitting
with me, and as time stretched on and on, I knitted
while waiting for service. None was offered that day
and we finally went away hungry. The next day the
St. Louis American printed a picture of me with the
caption, "Pregnant woman waits for service which
never came."

Charles Oldham became active in CORE through his involvement with the American Veterans Committee and
SCAN at Washington University. Now a St. Louis attorney, Oldham recalled in a 1995 interview how it all began:

Joe Ames, a CORE member, wandered into my office
and said, "Look, we're having a demonstration over
here at one of these stores. Why don't you come and
join us?"

I said, "Why, sure."

I just felt that something ought to be done and I was really disappointed in myself that I hadn't been more active. So when this opportunity came I started going to the meetings and demonstrations. I had no problem with CORE discipline at all. I thought it was something that people ought to consider adopting, in terms of their whole life structure.

We enjoyed it. We had a good time. We felt we were accomplishing something. When you combine a situation where you like what you're doing, where you have good relationships with the people you're doing it with, and when you're moving toward a goal, you get a lot of commitment.

While Norman Seay was a student at Vashon High School, he met Maggie Dagen through Intergroup Youth. In a 1995 interview, he recalled,

Apprehensively, I rode the streetcar, monthly, to attend discussion groups at Mrs. Dagen's home in University City. Bear in mind that an integrated group was a very rare phenomenon. I was always afraid that the police would stop me and question my motives for traveling to University City. Once I arrived at the Dagens' home, Mrs. Dagen would serve some nonalcoholic concoction, with cookies, while we sat and talked at ease.

I attended CORE meetings regularly. Being an integrated group during those times was, in my opinion, one of the odd but beautiful things about CORE. The group was comprised of Caucasians, Protestants, Jews, everything.

I have no interest in returning to Africa or a separate state in the United States, or living in a certain geographical area. That might have worked years ago. Today's world is too small for splinter groups or individuals espousing separatism. We need each other too much. We're all interrelated now.

After a CORE reunion at the home of Marian and Charles Oldham in August 1983, Mervene Ross returned to Washington, D.C., where she was president of D.C. University, and wrote to Maggie and Irv Dagen:

> Each one present that evening had incorporated much of the early CORE experience in their subsequent behavior, and attitudes. I am not sure you could have that same kind of evening in an un-self-conscious way, even if you tried to arrange it, for young people. The love and trust of the participants must grow through shared encounters and common concerns, generated through shared experience and the mutual respect that results. However, I do believe that there are young people with the openness and dedication who can and will come together. We did it in the late '40s. Other did it in the '60s. Hold your breath! It can and will happen again. Meanwhile, there are residuals from the good will of the '40s and '60s. After all, we are still around!

Ten

The Legacy, an Update

What a great feeling, to be involved with durable
friends in a noble cause.
> —Huston Smith

CORE had a huge influence in my life.
> —Walter Hayes

I grew up in CORE.
> —Billie Ames Teneau

Looking back after half a century, veterans of CORE's campaigns in the 1940s and 1950s had no difficulty recognizing their younger selves. Their responses to the questionnaire about CORE's influence in their later lives reflected a unanimous agreement that they had remained steadfastly committed to the values that had brought them together in a common cause. To a person, each would happily do it again.

Like soldiers in battle, they forged enduring friendships and a sense of mutual trust. They remembered the camaraderie of their Sunday picnics in Forest Park, where interracial groups had not been permitted or seen before. Billie Ames Teneau recalled that Marian Oldham's parents, Wanda Penny's mother, and Mervene Ross's mother baby-sat for her two small children while she demonstrated with CORE. Joyce and Steve Best, Walter and Burlee Hayes, Marian and Charles Oldham, and John and Vivian Olsen pioneered racially integrated housing, living in the Oldhams' four-family flat in north St. Louis.

CORE's style was simple. The weekly meetings were held first in an apartment and then in a church basement. There were no dues, ceremonies, banquets, awards, or special recognition. Social life consisted of an occasional whist tournament or bridge game, parties and visits in each other's homes, and, of course, the Sunday picnic-demonstrations. Members became close friends and found common interests. Skin color was regarded as no more significant than eye color. Walter Hayes spoke for many when he wrote, in 1995, "The only people more important to me during my early years with CORE were my family."

Charlie Oldham echoed this sentiment in an interview in 1995:

> The important things that came out of the CORE experience were the relationships we had with other individuals and the satisfaction we got from creating lifelong friendships that have endured. My marriage to Marian came directly out of the CORE experience and our recognition that race should not be a factor in interpersonal relationships.

Charles and Marian O'Fallon Oldham led lives of significant involvement and achievement in civil rights. Charles told how Marian honed her leadership skills in CORE:

> She learned those skills chairing CORE meetings. We were all talkative and had ideas and wanted to express them. At the same time, chairing a meeting and getting a program mapped out required some skill. Marian was excellent at it, and later, when she was on the board of curators at the University of Missouri and also on the boards of the New City School, John Burroughs School, and Community

School, she used those lessons and skills that she had learned in CORE. She always had a certain agenda that had to do with the admission of blacks to the school or the hiring of more blacks in jobs.

Charles recalled how Marian used her CORE skills to win over those who were antagonistic, including a member of the board of curators of the University of Missouri:

There was a fellow from Sikeston on the board of curators who was a typical Southern antagonist, and he became very fond of Marian. He started supporting her on issues involving the hiring of blacks, the awarding of contracts, and increasing the number of blacks who had tenure. Marian knew that remaining patient and calm and not being antagonistic and coming back and coming back would finally win the day.

Marian instituted a scholarship program for minority students at the University of Missouri–St. Louis, and long after she left the board of curators, she was so highly respected that faculty, administrators, and students from the university continued to call her for advice. Today, a bronze bust of Marian stands in the lobby of the Thomas Jefferson Library at the University of Missouri–St. Louis, keeping her memory alive.

Throughout his legal career, Charles Oldham has specialized in labor law and civil rights law. He has argued two cases before the U.S. Supreme Court. As a board member of the Annie Malone Children and Family Service Center and as chairman of the Marian Oldham Scholarship Fund at the University of Missouri–St. Louis, he is active in the support of education and social welfare. He believes that CORE techniques and the CORE point of view apply to all of life, "not only CORE projects, but also personal life and business affairs."

Marvin Rich, who also had an interracial marriage and was an early member of St. Louis CORE, stated that CORE was crucial in his life:

> It has affected my career. It has affected my life. It's where I chose to spend my life. I had some skills which I've used, fund-raising and writing and editing. . . . I make my financial contributions to organizations that make a difference on issues of race and class and gender. That's where my friends are. Those are my goals. I feel lucky that I grew up at that particular moment in time and that I had a particular group of friends, because I might have been completely different and self-satisfied. CORE has been crucial to me.
>
> I learned *My Experiments with Truth*, through Gandhi's autobiography, I sympathized, empathized, with it. It was not simply something that worked on a tactical level. I didn't know how you'd get it to work in a strategic sense. But I was comfortable with it. I would like to have made it work in a wider sphere, but I really believed that it could work in our community.

What held CORE together and kept it going despite opposition? According to Rich:

> The incentive was that we were doing something important, and we were all utterly convinced that it was important. We had huge opposition and we also had some success, and the combination of opposition and success was important in maintaining morale.

Underscoring his words was a statement in the October 1951 issue of *Up to Date with CORE:*

What Makes Us Tick?

We all have in common the belief that all men are equal regardless of skin color or ancestry. The system of racial segregation and the practice of racial discrimination have no rightful place in our city, our state, our court, or even in our world.

We also have in common the belief that violence can accomplish nothing in the struggle for civil and human rights. Every act of violence committed by minority groups pushes the goal of equality farther away into the distance. Under no circumstances, even when violence is directed toward us, do CORE people resort to violence. If we are persistent and continue our nonviolent action and passive resistance long enough, Jim Crow cannot win.

Walter Hayes also attributed a deep and lasting influence on his life to CORE:

CORE was a magnificent character developer. The organization instilled in me, and I am sure in others, a quiet inner strength, a clear sense of ethical values, and a determination to put them into practice and work for what you believe in. These values remain with me to this day.

When Walter Hayes applied for higher positions at the post office, he was passed over. Over time, the post office promoted five white applicants, less qualified and less experienced than he. In 1970 Hayes filed a discrimination suit against the United States Post Office. His attorneys were Charles Oldham and Louis Gilden. Hayes recalled,

It was the first time a person in a management position had filed a discrimination suit against . . . any government agency. It was a clear-cut case of flagrant discrimination that had been a long-standing practice.

We won the case, and created a better climate for blacks to get more promotions throughout the postal service. My CORE experience made me capable of taking this kind of action. In retrospect, CORE had a huge impact on my life.

For Billie Ames Teneau, editor of *Up to Date with CORE,* recruiter, coordinator, and participant in many tests and demonstrations, CORE was a "blessing":

> Those years in CORE had an important influence on my temperament. Of course, it is difficult to know what one would be like if the past had been differ- ent. But I feel those years in CORE had an important influence on my temperament. In CORE, the aim was to find that peaceful, non-violent approach; to always keep your cool; and to handle problems calmly. I grew up in CORE.

For thirty years, Billie worked in the Ferguson-Floris- sant School District, mainly as a teacher of drama. Her policy of using interracial casts was innovative and suc- cessful. After retiring from that district, she taught for more than five years in the St. Louis Public Schools at Marquette Visual and Performing Arts Middle School, where she continued her policy of interracial casting.

From the founding of CORE in 1947 through its first decade, Irv and Maggie Dagen were active in all of CORE's efforts. After a brief stint in Louisville, Kentucky, where both Irv and Maggie worked on interracial issues (Maggie helping to integrate the schools, Irv working on legal and labor relations issues), the Dagens returned to St. Louis and devoted much of their lives to education and civic betterment.

Irv expressed his commitment to integration, equality, and the peaceful means of bringing about social change in his practice of law and as general counsel of the St. Louis Hous- ing Authority and the St. Louis Redevelopment Authority. Irv pushed for integration of St. Louis governmental boards and commissions as well as equal employment opportunities throughout the community.

Maggie taught at Clayton High School, where she developed an innovative senior human relations course and organized a school-wide human relations club. She also taught labor relations at Washington University and short courses in that field throughout the country. Even though public schools were segregated by state law until after the 1954 Supreme Court decision, Maggie brought students of both races together in classes and extracurricular activities, gaining the support of parents and school administrators.

She involved her students in the Intergroup Youth Council, an area-wide interracial and interreligious organization, founded by Virgil Border, head of the National Conference of Christians and Jews; Myron Schwartz, head of the Jewish Community Relations Council; and faculty from Saint Louis University. In Intergroup Youth, African American and white high school teachers met with interracial groups of students several Saturdays a month to discuss current community issues and to plan an annual conference held each February, usually at Soldan High School in St. Louis. About fifteen hundred high school students from segregated black and white schools attended. They listened to prominent speakers, participated in discussion groups and other activities, and ate lunch together. Norman Seay was one of the high school students whose involvement in Intergroup Youth led to his involvement in CORE.

During this period, in the early 1950s, Maggie took her students from Clayton High School to meet Jackie Robinson, the first African American in major league baseball. The Brooklyn Dodgers were in town to play the St. Louis

Cardinals. While the white Dodger players stayed at an air-conditioned hotel with a swimming pool, the black players had to spend the hot summer nights at a hotel for blacks that did not have air conditioning. The students talked with Jackie Robinson for well over an hour and persuaded him to come to an all-school assembly the next day. He requested that the students invite a white player to come with him, so they asked Carl Erskine, the Dodger's star pitcher.

Thus began a longtime friendship and correspondence between Maggie and Jackie Robinson. She invited him to speak at the Intergroup Youth Brotherhood Conference and at other community, school, and youth groups in St. Louis and in Louisville, Kentucky. In Louisville, beloved baseball hero Pee Wee Reese, Dodger team captain, accompanied Robinson. On each occasion Robinson's powerful dignity and quiet courage had a strong impact on his listeners.

In 1963, Maggie Dagen became the associate director of admissions at Washington University. She said, "I looked out my office window in Brookings Hall for a couple of weeks and I never saw a single black student." During her eighteen years on the campus she worked constantly and creatively to change that scene, recruiting black students from high schools in Missouri and across the country, arranging financial aid and helping set up various support systems. She urged the integration of staff and faculty.

In his book *Washington University in St. Louis: A History,* Ralph E. Morrow credits Maggie with the initiation and continued efforts toward racial diversification on the campus. It was the realization of goals set by the American Veterans Committee and SCAN back in 1947. Maggie promoted diversity and effected change in many volunteer organizations.

Wanda Penny, an early member of CORE, died in 1994. Maggie aptly described her as "a beautiful, gracious, gentle woman who had the courage and discipline to become regularly involved in this pioneer activity. She helped convert resistance, hostility, and threats to change, and she even brought about friendships with our adversaries." Wanda Penny became an assistant professor of art at Harris-Stowe State College and later served as the head of the department of arts and science. She exerted a positive influence at the college and throughout the community toward improving human relations.

Steve Best went on to work for the Missouri Welfare Department. He was active with FOR, and he served on the board of the Lentz Peace Research Laboratory, directed by Ted Lentz, a Washington University psychologist who studied character and attitude development. In an interview Best remembered the influence of CORE on his life:

> Being in a successful movement like CORE was one of the major experiences of my life. In time, one could actually get results, as more and more public accommodations became integrated. Occasionally, I have become reacquainted with former CORE members: Norman Seay, Billie Teneau, Bill Clay, Marian and Charles Oldham, Walter Hayes, Henry Hodge. . . . Those people became a great influence on my personal and professional life.

Vernell Fuller became an attorney. He served for four years as the director of affirmative action for the State of Missouri and as a member of Governor Teasdale's cabinet. He believed that CORE made a unique contribution to human relations:

> I think the significant effect on the St. Louis area was that for the first time we had people like Maggie and

Billie and myself who were sitting there arm in arm, side by side, focused on a common goal that had never been focused on before. It proved that this could occur, that this should occur, and I think it was very persuasive. What other strategy could have been more effective?

Al Park, now a retired business executive, looked back on his participation in CORE:

What a moving experience was CORE. Beautiful people, working unselfishly, with very little conflict, in a most democratic environment. It truly was one of the memorable experiences of my life.

His wife, Ann Park, echoed his statement:

My experience in CORE was a very personal growth experience. Having grown up in a small Illinois town with a prejudiced mother and a bigoted father, this was my first exposure to blacks. Friendships were formed, stereotypical thinking began to dissolve, and out of this arrived a passion for civil rights, personal rights. Thanks to our friends, Irv and Maggie Dagen, we became involved in meetings, sit-ins, and picketing. The only scary time was an assignment to monitor a Gerald L. K. Smith meeting and be exposed to the hate.

In summary, CORE began my journey into more tolerance for all people, different or the same as I.

Norman Seay, a devoted member of CORE, became an educator and civil rights leader. He established the Dr. Martin Luther King Committee, which conducts a yearly commemoration of King's birthday. The committee was responsible for the renaming of Martin Luther King Boulevard and the Martin Luther King Bridge in St. Louis.

As director of the office of equal opportunity, Seay is an important influence on the campus of the University of Missouri–St. Louis among administrators, faculty, and students. In a 1995 interview he said,

> Everything I have accomplished in life was built upon preceding events. Marian Oldham, who became the first African American female on the University of Missouri's board of curators, recommended me to Marguerite Ross Barnett, the first African American chancellor of the University of Missouri–St. Louis, for my current position as director of the office of equal opportunity.

In the 1950s, Bonnie Marglous Rosen worked as program director for the Germantown Settlement in Philadelphia. She was responsible for the racial integration of that social welfare agency, and she worked with John McDermott, assistant director of the City of Philadelphia Commission on Human Relations, to avert conflict during the racial transition of the Germantown area of Philadelphia. From 1968 to 1980, she served as a Democratic Party committeewoman in Tippecanoe County, Indiana, and was vice chairman of the central committee for six years. She teaches English as a second language in the University City Adult Basic Education Program. Recalling her experience in CORE, she said:

> It seems to me that we did what had to be done in the best possible way, quietly, steadfastly, with good will and humor. The idea of respecting the reality of others, including those who do not agree with us, waiting patiently for them to change their practices, while we maintain our own separateness and dignity, demonstrating by our presence the certainty that all will be well when all are treated equally. That is as important now as it ever was. I find that the so-

called discipline of CORE is really the best way to
live.

As I review the CORE experience, I see it more as
a process than as an organization. The CORE approach is a whole-hearted application of the Golden
Rule.

Henry Hodge became chairman of the human relations
commission of the City of San Diego, California, and
chairman of the San Diego Citizen Law Enforcement Review Board. He learned much from his early involvement
in CORE. He wrote,

> From my first CORE meeting in 1947, I was
> launched into an era of civil rights and human rights
> activity that continues unabated to the present time.
> I was raised in midtown St. Louis, around the Wash-
> ington-Ewing area, which means I had all the think-
> ing and biases of that time plus the anger that all
> blacks felt. CORE provided me with a high degree of
> acceptance and a constructive outlet for addressing
> discriminatory practices.

Mary McClain completed her master of social work degree and married William McAllister, also a graduate
of the George Warren Brown School of Social Work. He
served as the secretary for boys' work at the then-segre-
gated Pine Street YMCA. He is now the president of the
International Association of Retired YMCA Executives.
Mary pursued her social work career in Minneapolis,
Chicago, and New York City. She recalled,

> At the sit-ins in St. Louis, long before the celebrated
> civil rights demonstrations, integration was taking
> place in St. Louis. There was no violence, no angry
> words, only well-disciplined white and black young
> people. We knew we were right and that our united

effort would one day overcome. I am proud to have in some small way contributed to the movement in St. Louis.

Before leaving St. Louis for Europe in 1950, Norman Winkler participated in many CORE demonstrations at Stix, Baer & Fuller. For many years he lived in Columbia, Maryland, an interracial community, where he became a leader in civic and cultural affairs. He wrote about it:

> Over the years, my convictions have not changed. In the 1960s, my wife and I chose to live in Columbia, Maryland, a planned, integrated community. And it has worked! Most residents of Columbia have stated that their principal reason for moving here was the open housing policy.

Irene Williams, who conducted the solo sit-in demonstration at Woolworth's when she was a student at Saint Louis University, wrote from Sitka, Alaska:

> My years working with CORE were a great source of new experience and new insights into the civil rights movement. It was also a time of meeting new friends, being exposed to new places and people and gaining valuable relationships that have continued to this day.

Remembering her years as a foot soldier in the 1950s, Vivian Dreer said in an interview:

> In reflecting on early CORE, I wondered how I happened to be interested in such an organization. Primarily, I found it appealing to use peaceful means to break the silence endured as we suffered indignities. CORE led an organized battle for human rights through demonstrations, without the conventional

bullets of warfare. It did so with an integrated army
representative of our American society.

Early members of CORE fought a good fight, but many
of them agree that the battle isn't over. Steve Best wrote,

> I am perturbed when I observe that our government
> often favors violent and confrontational last-resort
> solutions to international problems . . . while ignor-
> ing the possibilities of negotiation, compromise,
> conflict resolution and other nonviolent methods.
>   Of course, interracial conflict still exists, and more
> work needs to be done.

In 1996 Kendra Smith wrote of her CORE experience:

> Thinking back, I appreciate so much that the African
> American members of CORE took risks and opened
> themselves to genuine friendships with whites,
> something that our history still makes rare. I feel
> hopeful when I consider my daughters and grand-
> daughter and the diversity among their friends.
>   The movement toward racial equality moves
> more slowly than a sand dune, part of a far larger
> movement than we realized, and one that is far from
> over yet.

Dr. Huston Smith, former professor of philosophy at
Washington University and author of *The Religions of Man*,
a national best-seller, and many other writings on comparative religion, underscored his wife's words:

> CORE was an important part of our eleven years at
> Washington University, from 1947 to 1958. Our ac-
> tivities included sit-ins at restaurants, at least one
> swim-in with hecklers surrounding the pool, which
> despite the sweltering day was empty except for our
> interracial group, strategy meetings, and several

parties which packed our house on Waterman Avenue to capacity with high spirits. There were also some threatening calls in the middle of the night.

What a great feeling to be involved with durable friends in a noble cause. Much remains to be done, but for what needed to be done then, Kendra and I feel the satisfaction of having put our shoulders to the wheel. The spirit of CORE remains alive.

Epilogue

In the beginning, the words for CORE were firmness and truth. They echoed the word that Mahatma Gandhi had created for his movement of nonviolent resistance to oppression: *satyagraha, sat* for truth, and *agraha* for firmness.

From 1947 to 1957, a unique interracial company of people waged a struggle in the city of St. Louis with truth and firmness, but without violence. They made visible what had so long been denied, and they tenaciously pursued their program of equality. The goal was audacious, the commitment courageous. By the end of the decade, CORE had opened a large number of once-segregated public accommodations, garnering understanding and support along the way from many who initially had been adversaries.

The reader could well wonder why, fifty years after the founding of St. Louis CORE, a small group of early CORE members searched out other scattered early members and gathered their memories to tell the story of those early years. It was because little had been written about early CORE, and little was saved. The early members had not been self-conscious about making history, only making change. Now the early members were aging and dying, and there might otherwise be no record to mark their ten-year effort.

The small group of early CORE members wished to pass on the legacy of their brief, but important, story. To those who would address seemingly intractable problems, their story offers an example of success against great odds and a message of hope and encouragement.

APPENDIX 1

Vol. I, No. 4   JUNE, 1951

UP TO DATE

WITH   CORE

Committee of Racial Equality
3403 Rex Avenue
St. Louis 14, Missouri   WInfield 4905

ALL IS WELL AT KATZ

The two-year campaign to open eating facilities in the Katz Drug stores to all races has reached the stage where the management of Katz is allowing an interracial group to be served once a week. Mr. S. A. Francis, District Manager of Katz, is notified by CORE just when the tests will take place. The purpose of the tests, of course, is to give the store officials an opportunity to observe customer reactions.

The first of these tests took place on May 7th. Wanda Penny and Margaret Dagen were served without incident. The same two CORE members were given prompt service on May 14th.

On May 28, Marion O'Fallon and Maggie were ignored and not served. An older fellow who had not been there the two previous weeks was managing the counter. The young fellow who had been managing the counter said he would like to serve the CORE members but he could not do it. The older fellow was not well liked by the other employees. One employee was heard to say that she wished he had stayed on his vacation indefinitely.

The next day, Maggie telephoned Mr. Francis and told him what had happened. Mr. Francis was very apologetic. He said there had been an accident in the store and that the manager of the store had not been available when the CORE members were there. Mr. Francis said he would talk with the employees.

On May 28, Marion and Maggie were given prompt service. The older fellow did not speak or look at them. The customers seemed completely undisturbed by Marian's presence.

Maggie has written to Mr. Shlensky in Kansas City to find out what impressions the Katz officials have about the tests that have been made.

NEAR VIOLENCE
AT POPE'S

On Friday, May 11, Joe Ames talked with Mr. Harry Pope on the telephone. Mr. Pope was still disturbed by the first demonstration which had been held in his restaurant on May 5. He said that all the demonstrations in the world would not change his policy.

On Saturday, May 12, seven CORE members stood in the Pope's Cafeteria line. A store employee stood in front of them so they could not move beyond the trays. White customers moved around the CORE group. Charles Oldham went outside to instruct any white CORE members who might be coming to the demonstration late. He was able to talk with Bill Richards before he entered the Cafeteria. Charlie and Bill went around the CORE group, stopped in front of the meat counter and then identified themselves with CORE. The waitress told Mr. Pope who turned to Charlie and said, "I want you to get out of here."

- 2 -

Pope took Charlie's tray, and Charlie kept the silver. Then Pope came back, took the silver, held Charlie by the arm and shoved him. Charlie and Bill then moved and stood at the end of the line of CORE people. When outside, Charlie had reached Eleanor Smith by telephone and instructed her to come down and go around the CORE group, then identify herself with CORE. She did this and told the waitress that she planned to share her food with with one of the colored CORE members. Mr. Pope took her tray and said that if she did not move he would use force. After he said it twice, Eleanor moved behind the other CORE people. One employee hit Mary Washington with his elbow and called her a "stupid thing". Mr. Pope told the employee to be more careful. The employee was courteous after that.

A few days later, Huston Smith tried to talk with Mr. Pope in person but was able to reach him only by telephone. A demonstration had been planned for the next day but, since Huston had not been able to speak with Mr. Pope in person, Huston told Pope the demonstration would be called off if he would agree to speak with several members of CORE the next day, May 19. Pope agreed to this and spoke with Joe, Huston, Charlie and Leo Stevens the next morning. Mr. Pope invited two plainclothes policemen to sit in on this discussion. Mr. Pope said he thought there would be a law passed soon to force all eating places to serve Negroes. He said the St. Louis Council on Human Relations should call a group of the restaurant owners together and get them to agree to open. Pope said he would appear before the Council and would write a letter asking the Council to work on the restaurant situation. Mr. Pope said that CORE was using unlawful tactics. He handed each CORE representative a copy of an ordinance and copies of Illinois decisions--none of which, in the opinion of CORE's lawyers, applied in this situation. Mr.

Pope again refused the once-a-week plan.

KRESGE'S

On May 9, 1951, a letter was mailed to Mr. H. D. Skayton, Manager of the Kresge Dime Store at 522 Washington where several sit-in demonstrations have been held. The letter reviewed what had happened at Kresge's and assured Mr. Skayton that even though demonstrations had been held in his store, CORE is still eager to settle the problem through discussion if at all possible. The letter further stated that to show our sincerity in wanting to solve the problem through discussion, we were temporarily discontinuing our demonstrations and that Billie Ames would telephone him within a few days to secure an appointment for a CORE representative to speak with him.

On May 14, Billie talked with Mr. Skayton by telephone and arranged for two CORE representatives to speak with him on the following Friday.

On May 18, Al Park and Irvin Dagen went to Mr. Skayton's office but were told that he was out of town. A Mr. Chandler, Merchandise Manager from Detroit was there to speak with the CORE representatives. Mr. Chandler know nothing about the situation, did not know about the demonstrations, had not read the letter CORE sent to Mr. Skayton, and had no power to do anything about the situation. Mr. Chandler said he would take any information Al and Irv could give him back to Detroit and discuss it with Mr. Fairbanks who is in charge of public relations. Al and Irv told him that arrangement was not satisfactory and that they would like to talk with Mr. Fairbanks. Mr. Chandler said he thought this would be possible since Mr. Fairbanks is frequently in this area.

- 3 -

On May 24, a letter was written to Mr. Fairbanks asking for an appointment to speak with him in St. Louis. There has been no answer to this letter.

FORUM COMPLICATIONS

On May 7th, Joe Ames talked with Mr. R. B. Tabler, manager of the Forum Cafeteria. Mr. Tabler said the CORE demonstrations were not reducing the number of customers but that the size of the checks was smaller because customers were not buying salads. (CORE people usually stood in front of the salad section during the demonstrations.)

A friend of CORE's who works in Chancellor Compton's office at Washington University reported that Mr. Tabler came out to see Chancellor Compton in the hope that Compton would do something to stop Washington University students from participating in CORE demonstrations at Forum. Mr. Tabler did not get to speak with Chancellor Compton but did talk to the girls in the office. They pointed out to him that only one of the names he had was that of a Washington University student. The girls suggested he stop the demonstrations in his cafeteria by serving Negroes.

A week later, Sandy Brent, a Washington University student who had been on a few CORE demonstrations, was called to the office of Dean Arno Haack. Forum management had written to Washington University enclosing three names and asking that something be done to stop these students from participating in CORE demonstrations at Forum. Again, only one of the names was that of a student. Sandy told the Dean about CORE and about the demonstrations. Dean Haack decided this was not a matter of concern to the University since CORE is not a campus organization.

On May 24, a letter was written to Mr. Hayman, President of Forum Cafeterias, Inc., telling him that demonstrations had not been held in the Forum during the last few weeks in the hope we would get further word from him. (In his letter of March 27th, Mr. Hayman had said he would be coming to St. Louis in "the very near future" and that he would be glad to discuss the situation with a CORE representative.) The letter further stated that if we did not have an opportunity to speak with him within the next week or ten days, we believed we must again use direct nonviolent action. There has been no answer to this letter.

A large demonstration was planned for June 2. A great deal of time and effort was spent in getting participants. The fact that there was going to be a large demonstration on June 2nd was published in the St. Louis Argus. The article suggested that anyone interested in participating telephone Billie Ames to get further information. Several people responded to this suggestion and were given full details about the demonstration. After full information concerning the demonstration had been mailed out, we realized that the address of one of the people who had spoken with Billie on the telephone was that of the Christian Nationalist Party (the Gerald L. K. Smith group). By the numerous detailed questions that had been asked, it was apparent that the Christian Nationalist Party members planned to participate in the June 2nd demonstration. Since the Christian Nationalist Party is organized for the purpose of promoting racial segregation, there was no doubt that the CN members would make every effort to nullify any progress CORE had been able to make at the Forum and in the downtown area. Consequently, the demonstration was called off on May 31 by telephone.

- 4 -

Three CORE members, Marvin Rich, Charles Oldham, and Joe Ames, stood in front of the Forum on June 2nd to turn away any demonstrators who may not have heard of the cancellation. About fifteen Christian Nationalist Party members were also there. CORE had notified the police of the reasons for cancelling the demonstration. The police were there but stayed for only half an hour. When it became apparent to the CN people that the demonstration had been called off, they started talking to the three white CORE members in very foul language and waving clubs made of tightly rolled magazines tied in several places with string. One of these magazines was rolled around a pipe. One CN member kicked Joe. Shortly after the police left, the CORE members decided to leave. Marvin and Joe were followed by two of the CN people. As the CORE members got on the street car, Marvin was hit two hard blows on the back and on the back of his neck with one of the rolled-up magazines. Marvin managed to say, "Excuse me" and stumbled back to a seat.

Shortly after this incident, the man who had asked for information about the demonstration and had given the address of the Christian Nationalist Party as his address, telephoned Billie and very innocently asked what had happened to the demonstration. He did not get any information this time. During the next few days, several CORE members were telephoned about six times—usually about 2:00 A.M.--and told, among other things, that they were nigger-lovers and Communist-Jews. The CORE members lives and persons were also threatened. One of the people who called said he was representing the Ku Klux Klan.

On Monday, June 4, Al Park and Charles Oldham talked with Mr. Tabler in his office. They told him what sort of group the Christian Nationalist Party is and showed him the name of the Party on the

Attorney General's list of subversive organizations. Mr. Tabler seemed to know nothing about the group but said he would make an effort to keep them out of the cafeteria. Mr. Tabler admitted he had been out at Washington University. He also agreed that Mr. Hayman had been very uncooperative with CORE.

WOOLWORTH NEGOTIATIONS

Irvin Dagen talked with Mr. Brelin, Southwest Regional Manager of Public Relations for Woolworth's, for two hours on May 14th The plan Mr. Brelin had been investigating in Kansas City had been a plan whereby the end of one counter would be opened to Negroes. Of course, Irv told him this would be completely unsatisfactory to CORE. Mr. Brelin said he had witnessed Negroes eating in a Walgreen's Drug Store and a Chippewa Drug Store (both within a couple of blocks of the new Woolworth store on Grand) and that there was no trouble. Mr. Brelin spoke with several of the Negroes who said they were glad to have a convenient place to eat Mr. Brelin also spoke with the managers of the two stores and they reported no trouble. The manager of the Chippewa Drug Store said a couple of his employees quit their jobs but that they had no trouble finding other employees to take their places. Mr. Brelin spoke with Mr. Young, manager of the new Woolworth store, and found that he had no objections to serving Negroes. Armed with this information, Mr. Brelin spoke with Mr. Deichmiller, district manager of Woolworth's. Mr. Deichmiller was almost convinced but backed out at the last minute. Mr. Brelin said he would talk with Mr. Deichmiller again soon and then call Irv.

On June 8, Irv spoke with Mr. Brelin on the telephone. Mr. Brelin said he had presented the

- 5 -

case to Mr. Deichmiller again but had received no answer yet. Mr. Brelin also said there is to be a large meeting in New York this month at which the problem of racial discrimination will probably be discussed.

ST. LOUIS COUNCIL ON HUMAN RELATIONS

On June 6, a letter was mailed to Mr. George W. Cloyd, Chairman of the St. Louis Council on Human Relations telling of the Christian Nationalist intervention and suggesting that the Council appoint a committee to work toward ending racial discrimination in restaurants and cafeterias in the downtown area and to help avoid a reoccurrence of violence by the Christian Nationalist group. This does not mean that CORE is abandoning work in the downtown area but, rather, that CORE is broadening the means by which we are trying to end racial discrimination. CORE is making an effort to get several restaurant managers to write letters to the Council asking for their help in solving the problem.

PAST HISTORY

Some of the people receiving UP-TO-DATE have been added to our mailing list since the first issue was mailed March, 1951. The March, April and May issues contained articles about the history of negotiations and demonstrations at Kresge's, Pope's Cafeteria, Forum Cafeteria, F-E Food Shops, Woolworth's Dime Store, and Teutenberg's. We will be glad to mail copies of the past issues to people interested in knowing what CORE action preceded that which is reported in this issue. Just telephone or write to the CORE office.

DOING YOUR DUTY?

Maybe you are eating regularly in the eating places now open for Negro patronage; maybe you are telling your friends that Negroes may now eat in the places listed below; maybe you are actually taking your colored friends with you to eat in these places--but if you are, it's news to us. All we know is that a few Negro CORE members are eating in these places and that we seldom see other Negroes eating there--particularly in those places marked with an asterisk. So eat out regularly--it's too hot to cook anyway. Then let us know you are using these facilities. Writ a post-card to CORE, 3433 Rex, o telephone Billie Ames at WInfiel 4905.

*Teutenberg's   320 N. Sixth
*Teutenberg's   714 Washington
*All Walgreen Drug Stores
*Chippewa Drug Store
    Grand & Washington
*Chippewa Drug Store
    Grand & St. Louis
*Sears, Roebuck and Co.
    Grand and Chippewa
*Sears, Roebuck and Co.
    Kingshighway & Easton
 E. St. Louis Bus Terminal
    4th & Washington
 Scruggs' Basement Cafeteria
    10th & Olive
 Downtown YMCA & YWCA
    Locust between 14th & 16th
 Municipal Art Museum Cafeteria
    Forest Park
 Fred Harvey Restaurant
    Union Station
 Schneithorst's Restaurant
    Lambert Field Airport

MEETINGS

You are welcome to attend our regular CORE meetings every Tuesday at 8:00 PM in the basement of the Centennial Christian Church located at Fountain and Aubert.

Vol. I, No. 5

JULY, 1951

UP TO DATE

W I T H   C O R E

Committee of Racial Equality
3403 Rex Avenue
St. Louis 14, Missouri

WInfield 4905

RECENT TACTICS

As was reported in the June issue of UP-TO-DATE, on June 2 members of the Christian Nationalist Party (the Gerald L. K. Smith group) accosted three CORE members in front of the Forum Cafeteria and abused them with foul language, kicks and blows with rolled-up magazines. For a short time following this incident, no CORE demonstrations were held at the Forum Cafeteria. Short demonstrations were held in several other downtown eating places. The St. Louis Council on Human Relations has appointed a committee to work for the ending of racial discrimination in the restaurants of the downtown area. The purpose of the short demonstrations held in several small eating places was to make them more aware of the problem and more receptive when approached by the Human Relations Council.

Forum demonstrations were resumed on July 2. At a Forum demonstration on July 9, Christian Nationalists were again present, and one CORE member and one Christian Nationalist member were arrested.

MISS JULIA'S

Miss Julia's Cafeteria is located at 120 N. 7th St. and is a small cafeteria having about twenty tables on the main floor and also an elevated floor in the rear.

Marion O'Fallon and Eleanor Smith ate at Miss Julia's in the spring of 1950. While they were eating the manager asked them to come back and talk with him when they finished their meal. During the discussion the manager, Mr. Patterson, brought out a large scrap-book showing the progress of their business and the struggle he and his wife had had in building it. He said he could not afford to serve Negroes because he would lose his white customers. When Marion and Eleanor explained about CORE, Mr. Patterson said that if CORE ever had any demonstrations in his cafeteria he would have to fire all his Negro employees.

Several weeks later, Marion and Eleanor were served again. Mr. Patterson told them Negroes would not be served there anymore.

Several more test groups composed of CORE members other than Marion and Eleanor were served during the next few months.

A test group was refused service in October of 1950. Marion talked with Mr. Patterson and invited him to a CORE-arranged managerial meeting which was held on November 9th, 1950. He said he would attend but did not.

About a week later, Walter Hayes and Al Park tried to eat at Miss Julia's. They were stopped before they got their trays full. Al and Walter spoke with Mr. Patterson for about an hour and presented the once-a-week plan whereby one interracial group would be served in Miss Julia's

- 2 -

once a week at a time prearranged
by CORE and Mr. Patterson. He
would not consider the plan. He
said there were several employees
working in offices in the building
who refused to eat in the cafeteria
if Mr. Patterson served anymore
Negroes. He said these people also
were trying to get him to fire his
Negro employees. At this time,
CORE was trying to arrange for a
CORE representative to speak before
the Restaurant Association. Al and
Walter asked Mr. Patterson if he
would help us get before the Assn.
He said that if he had an opportunity to vote on it secretly, he would
vote in CORE's behalf. He also
said he would be willing to open
his facilities if all the other eat-
places did too. Walter and Al invited Mr. Patterson to attend
another CORE-arranged managerial
meeting to be held in one of Thompson's Restaurants on February 8th,
1951. Again he said he would attend, but he did not.

On June 30, 1951, Mary Rieser
and Wanda Penny left Miss Julia's
after being refused service. A few
minutes later Henry Hodge, Steve
Best, Orvell French and Joe Ames
walked into the cafeteria. The
police, whom CORE had notified,
must have told Mr. Patterson because
he seemed prepared for the CORE
group. The trays had been moved
from the counter so the CORE people
could not get them. (Mr. Patterson
handed the trays to other customers
who went around the CORE group.)
When told that colored people are
not served in the Cafeteria, the
CORE group said they would wait.
The manager took their names. Mr.
Patterson asked an employee to bring
him the time-cards of the colored
employees and said,"If they're going
to do this, I'll fire the whole
damned bunch of them." He took the
time-cards and figured out how much
money each Negro employee was to
receive. The CORE group left after
standing 45 minutes. As they were
leaving, Joe stopped and talked with
Mr. Patterson. Patterson said he
had cooperated in every way he could.

He said he had not attended the
managerial meetings because nobody else had come. He insisted
he was going to fire his colored
employees. Joe told him that
such action would simply mean
CORE would have to single out
Miss Julia's as the one eating
place we were to concentrate on
and that we would have demonstrations there frequently.

On July 6, Norman Seay talked
with Mr. Patterson for thirty
minutes. At this time we were
suggesting that managers write
letters to the St. Louis Council
on Human Relations asking that
the Council try to help settle
the problem of racial discrimination. (CORE had sent such a letter and one manager, Mr. Pope,
had written one.) Mr. Patterson
said he would not write such a
letter. He again said he would
not accept the once-a-week plan.
He said that CORE could put him
out of business in two weeks. He
said a loss of one hundred regular customers would mean he would
have to close the cafeteria. He
seemed to have no confidence in
what CORE members said and believed the white people in CORE
simply were using the colored members. Mr. Patterson complained
that the several times he had
served CORE people, they had always sat in conspicuous places
rather than going to the back.
He said he would probably open
his facilities if Forum, Hulling'
Pope's, and Thompson's Cafeterias
were opened to Negroes. Norman
suspects that his conversation
with Mr. Patterson was recorded.
(Mr. Patterson turned on a switch
when Norman walked in and turned
it off when Norman left.)

SHOPPERS' LUNCH

Shoppers' Lunch, 720 Locust,is
a small lunch counter with about
twenty-five seats. There are
also about three tables on the
first floor and a very small balcony.

- 3 -

In the spring of 1950, Jerry Parnas and Henry Hodge were served at the counter in Shoppers' Lunch. A week later, Rose Parnas and Marion O'Fallon were served. Joe Ames observed both these tests. After the second group was served, Joe heard the manager say that they should have put poison in the sandwiches. One of the waitresses scolded the waiter who served the CORE members.

Two weeks later Rose and Wanda Penny entered the restaurant at 5:30 pm, sat at the counter and were ignored. They continued waiting in their seats. By seven o'clock, the other customers had left. Only the two CORE members, the manager--Mr. Harry Gagliarbi, and a waiter remained in the restaurant. Mr. Gagliarbi told the waiter to stay there while he went out to find a policeman. When he came back, he said he could find no policeman and told the waiter to go home. Mr. Gagliarbi then went upstairs leaving the two CORE members alone on the first floor. After about fifteen minutes, one of the CORE members said, "Won't you come down and talk with us?" He came down and admitted he was the manager. (Up until then he had given an evasive answer when asked who the manager was.) He blamed his refusal to serve Negroes on his employees whom he said would not serve colored people. He agreed to come to the next managerial meeting on November 9th, 1950, but did not. He fixed Wanda a sandwich and the two CORE members left. (Wanda thinks she could have eaten the sandwich there, but they both had other engagements so they left taking the sandwich with them.)

After Mr. Gagliarbi failed to attend the November 9th meeting, CORE held a small sit-in demonstration lasting for an hour. By this time, Mr. Gagliarbi had posted a sign which said, "We reserve the right to refuse service to anyone." He ignored the CORE group.

A few days later Wanda talked with Mr. Gagliarbi and said she was very disappointed that he had not attended the last managerial meeting, and that she hoped she would be able to tell the CORE group that he certainly would attend the next one. He promised to attend the meeting of Feb. 8, 1951 and did attend. However, very little was accomplished because representatives from only two eating places were there.

Several weeks later, Wanda spoke with Mr. Gagliarbi and tried to get him to accept the once-a-week plan. He said he would accept it only if the other restaurant managers did too.

On June 9th, an interracial group of seven CORE people continued sitting at the counter after being refused service. Billie Ames, Mary Rieser and Sallie Heller were observing the demonstration. The police took the names of the demonstrators and two of the observers (Mary and Sallie) whom were recognized by one of the waitresses. Then Mr. Gagliarbi closed his restaurant. The CORE group and the two observers left and waited across the street. Billie continued sitting, eating and talking with other customers who had already been served and with the employees. Mr. Gagliarbi kept his restaurant closed the rest of the day. (It was 2:00 pm when the CORE group left.) He thought that serving white people after refusing to serve the Negroes would give us basis for bringing suit against him. He was afraid to have the CORE group arrested for fear we would arrest him on peace disturbance charges. The manager and the employees seemed to think they would lose more money by serving Negroes than by closing the restaurant when the CORE group came in. The waitress who recognized Sallie and Mary as CORE members felt like a heroine and

- 4 -

thought she should be put on the police force.

On June 23, four CORE people sat and waited for an hour after being refused service at Shoppers' Lunch. This time Mr. Gagliarbi did not close the restaurant and completely ignored the CORE group.

On July6, Wanda spoke with Mr. Gagliarbi again and asked him to cooperate by writing a letter to the St. Louis Council on Human Relations asking them to help in solving the problem of racial discrimination in the downtown area. Mr. Gagliarbi readily agreed to do this.

BLACK CAT CAFETERIA

The Black Cat Cafeteria at 910 Olive has about forty tables and a twelve-seat counter on the main floor and a small balcony.

In the spring of 1950, Marvin Rich, Augustus Bell, and Irvin Dagen were refused service. Gus talked with the manager, Mr. Geo. Mavramadus, several times in person and on the telephone. Gus invited him to the meeting of November 9th, but he did not attend. At one point, Mr. Mavramadus tried to break off negotiations completely.

Several weeks after the Nov. 9 meeting, a small demonstration was held at the counter on the main floor. Nine CORE people participated. Mr. Mavramadus told each colored person individually that he would not be served. Joe Ames tried to talk with him. He said he would talk with Joe if all the demonstrators left. Joe would not agree to such an arrangement. Then Mr. Mavramadus told Joe to follow him and then they would talk. Joe supposed they were going to Mr. Mavramadus' office, but they ended up down in the basement between two garbage cans. Mavramadus said the mayor and the churches should solve this problem of racial discrimination. He promised to

attend the next managerial meeting on February 8. The CORE group left after about thirty minutes.

Joe talked with him again before the Feb. 8th meeting and Mr Mavramadus again said he would attend but he did not.

About five weeks ago, Steve Best and Joe talked with the manager. Mr. Mavramadus had no explanation for not having attended the managerial meeting as he had promised. He would not consider the once-a-week plan. Joe and Steve told him that we may decide to have more demonstrations since he refused to try the once-a-week plan.

A demonstration took place on June 9, 1951. Seven CORE people stood in the cafeteria line. Sallie Heller, Mary Rieser and Billie Ames observed. Mr. Mavramadus' first remark was "Hello there, trying something new?" Shortly after that, he called th police. (CORE had failed to notify the police of the demonstration.) The police told Mavramadus that they could arrest us if he wanted them to but that they could not make us move. Mr. Mav ramadus tried to get the CORE group to move back so customers could go in front of them. The CORE group did not move. He then sent customers around the CORE group which left after about 30 minutes. There were twelve policemen, a patrol wagon, a squad car, a prowl car with two detectives and a police capt. in a car outside the Cafeteria.

On June 23, six CORE people stood in the cafeteria line for forty minutes. Two employees stood between the CORE group and the trays. Mr. Mavramadus spoke to the group only once when he said, "Hello". CORE had notified the police this time, and only about three policemen were there.

- 5 -

EXCITEMENT AT FORUM

After our experiences with the
Christian Nationalists on June 2
and the talk Charles Oldham and Al
Park had with Mr. Tabler, Manager
of Forum Cafeteria, no further action was taken at Forum for several
weeks.

On July 2, ten CORE people stood
in the line and Joe Ames passed out
leaflets outside the cafeteria.
There were many comments against
management and about twelve people
left without eating. This time an
employee stood outside the railing
where he could direct customers a-
round the CORE group without having to talk loudly. This system,
however, also put him in a more
convenient position to receive customer complaints. One man complained in a loud voice and attracted the attention of other customers. As the man berated the
employee for refusing to serve
Negro customers when Negro soldiers
were dying on the battle fields
overseas, one woman banged her
spoon on the table and said, "This
man is not responsible for this."
The man swore a little and left.
Later two young fellows came in
with their dates. When they saw
what was going on, the fellows
joined the stand-in and the girls
went outside. One of the fellows
offered to buy Adolph Price some
food. The CORE group stayed an
hour and then left.

On July 7th, seven CORE people
stood in the Forum line for an hour.
Marvin Rich passed out leaflets
outside the cafeteria.   Two fellows
from a near-by store spent their
entire lunch hour joining in the
demonstration. One rough-looking
man in work clothes came in, knocked
several girl demonstrators aside
with his elbows and put his tray
between theirs. Mr. Tabler told
him that he wanted no violence in
the cafeteria and that he rather
not have the man's business. The
man continued walking in the line.

On July 9th, ten CORE people
stood in the Forum line for an
hour (6:00 pm 'til 7:00 pm). Joe
distributed leaflets outside. As
usual, CORE had notified the
police. One policeman stood with
in twenty feet of Joe most of the
time Joe was there. A squad car
drove by several times. About
6:30 the policeman walked away
and the squad car drove away a-
round the corner--at that moment
a Christian Nationalist station
wagon with three people drove up.
Two young fellows jumped out and
one of them asked for a leaflet
which Joe gave him. The man in
the station wagon, Don Lohbeck,
yelled, "Take them all. If he
won't give them to you, take them
anyway." So one of the young
fellows, Clark, grabbed the leaflets. Joe hung on for a second
but then let loose because he did
not want to start a fight. Clark
threw the leaflets into the station wagon. Lohbeck told the
fellows to go inside the cafeteria
and get that "lousy little kike
with the glasses". (He was re-
ferring to Marvin Rich who was no
participating in this demonstration.) Joe walked half a block
and told the traffic policeman
that it looked like there was going to be a fight in the Forum.
At that moment the squad car which
had just driven around the block
appeared and the traffic policeman
sent the car to the Forum. The
two fellows ran in, talked with
the employee directing customers
around the CORE group, stepped
over the railing and ran up the
stairs apparently in search of the
manager. They soon came down the
stairs and talked with the Assistant Manager, Mr. Raidt. One
man from the squad car, the traffic policeman, and Joe came in and
found the fellows. The police
told Joe to go outside and wait.
A few minutes later the police
came out of the cafeteria with the
two fellows. Joe and the two fellows were taken to the police station. The squad car had pursued

- 6 -

and caught Lohbeck who had driven
away in the station wagon. He, too,
was taken to the police station.
Clark kept yelling that he wanted
Joe arrested for littering the side
walk with leaflets. Joe told the
policeman that he wasn't sure he
wanted to have Clark arrested. The
policeman said the judge could decide weither or not the fellow
should be arrested. Joe and Clark
were booked, put in separate cells,
bailed out and told to appear in
police court the following morning.

The demonstrators inside the
cafeteria did not know just what
was going on outside. They continued standing in line until 7:00--
the usual time for leaving. When
the CORE people came out, Joe, the
Christian Nationalists and the
police were gone. There were many
antagonistic remarks noted during
this demonstration. One man handed
a card to an employee and said in a
loud voice, "Give this to the manager. Tell him I'm on his side."
Another man loudly said, "That's
right, keep it up. Continue what
you are doing. This is the way you
make people hate each other." A
man and woman went through the line
twice making antagonistic remarks.

On July 10, Joe and Clark appeared in court. Clark lied several times on the stand. When Joe's
lawyer, Mark Hennelly, asked Clark
if he was a member of the Christian
Nationalist Party, Clark said he
wanted to get a lawyer. The case
is to be continued on July 23rd.
The prosecuting attorney said Clark
had no valid charges against Joe.
After the postponement of the trial,
Clark came up to Joe and said, "The
boss says we'll drop our case if
you'll drop yours." Joe suggested
he send his lawyer to talk it over.
A news release given out by the
Christian Nationalists was printed
in the Globe-Democrat. The column
was about two and a half inches
long and was headlined, "Two in
Scuffle Over Handbills Arrested".

KRESGE'S

There has been no response to
our letter of May 24th to Mr.
Fairbanks asking for an opportunity to speak with him. Mr. Fairbanks is in charge of public relations for the Kresge stores and
has his office in Detroit.

On June 29th, Billie Ames tele
phoned Mr. Skayton, manager of the
downtown Kresge's dime store in
which we have held several sit-in
demonstrations, and asked if we
could have an appointment for a
CORE representative to speak with
him. He said no--it would be a
waste of time since the situation
is now in the hands of Mr. Fairbanks. Billie told him we had
received no reply to our last letter to Mr. Fairbanks and asked Mr
Skayton what he suggested we do--
wait longer for a response or
write another letter. Mr. Skayton
said it was possible that the last
letter had been misplaced, and he
suggested we write another one.

Another letter was written to
Mr. Fairbanks on July 2 saying
that CORE was continuing to post-
pone public demonstrations at
Kresge's in the hope that we would
soon be able to talk with him here
in St. Louis.

CORE CONVENTION

The annual CORE Conference-
Convention was held at Camp Joy
near Cincinnati from June 14-17.
During the first three days, CORE
representatives from many parts of
the country discussed their local
problems and exchanged ideas.

The Convention started Friday
evening and lasted through Sunday
morning. The following CORE
groups were represented: Cincin-
nati, Ohio; Minneapolis, Minn.;
Pasadena, Calif.; Washington, D.C.
New York, N.Y.; Chicago, Ill.;
Evanston, Ill.; and St. Louis, Mo.
St. Louis was represented by Janet
Thompson, Billie and Joe Ames, and

- 7 -

Marvin Rich. The following officers
were elected for the coming year:
Executive Director, George Houser of
New York; Chairman, Billie Ames of
St. Louis; Vice Chairman, Lynn Kirk
of Washington; Secretary, Lorraine
Edelen of Evanston; Treasurer,
Catherine Raymond of New York. Field
Representatives for the coming year
will be Marian Coddington of Pasadena, Wallace Nelson of Cincinnati,
Harriett Lane of Minneapolis and A.
C. Thompson of Evanston. The Convention delegates agreed unanimously
to ask Mr. Harold J. Gibbons, head
of the AFL Teamsters Union, Local
688, in St. Louis to be on CORE's
advisory committee.

MANPOWER

In reading this issue, you probably have observed that the number
of people who participate in the
CORE demonstrations is small. Even
the small groups are effective.
However, the effectiveness of our
demonstrations could be greatly in-
creased if more people would parti-
pate. We need your help. Participate in the demonstrations if you
possibly can.

NEW OFFICERS

On July 10, at the regular CORE
meeting the following people were
elected to serve as officers for
the next three months: Sallie
Heller, President; Irvin Dagen, Vice
President and Chairman of the Mem-
bership Committee; Margie Humphrey,
Recording Secretary; Billie Ames,
Corresponding Secretary; and Wanda
Penny, Treasurer. The Membership
Committee will consist of Irvin
Dagen as Chairman, Marvin Rich,
Walter Hayes, Charles Oldham, and
Edgar Poindexter.

MEETINGS

You are welcome to attend our
regular CORE meetings every Tuesday
at 8:00 PM in the basement of the
Centennial Christian Church located
at Fountain and Aubert Sts.

PLEASE TAKE NOTE

Some of you who receive
copies of UP-TO-DATE may want to
have parts of it printed in
other publications. Please do
not do so without the consent of
St. Louis CORE. For tactical
reasons, some of the information
given in issues of UP-TO-DATE
should not receive wide publicity. Please telephone Billie
Ames at Winfield 4905 or write
to the CORE office before re-
printing any part of the information given in the issues of
UP-TO-DATE. We will appreciate
your cooperation.

STICK YOUR NECK OUT

Yes, if your skin is dark it
takes a lot of nerve to go into
eating places which have been
open for white customers only
for so many years. But times
have changed--the places listed
below do serve Negroes and have
served them many times. CORE
members eat in these places frequently in both all-Negro and
interracial groups. If you do
not see any colored people eating in these places, eat there
anyway and urge your friends to
eat there, too. True, you may
not get ideal service. We find
some waitresses serve slowly and
inefficiently regardless of the
customer's color. Then, too, you
may find some waitresses who do
give inferior service only to
colored persons. But the best
way to eliminate this tendency
is to eat in these places frequently if you are colored so
the waitresses will become used
to serving Negroes. Leaving a
tip also helps to convert an antagonistic waitress. Make a
special effort to eat in at least
the places marked with an asterisk. These places have been
opened to Negroes recently and
receive little Negro patronage.
(List of restaurants given
on the back of this sheet.)

- 8 -

*Teutenberg's	320 N. Sixth
*Teutenberg's	714 Washington

*All Walgreen Drug Stores
*Chippewa Drug Store
    Grand & Washington
*Chippewa Drug Store
    Grand & St. Louis
*Sears, Roebuck and Company
    Grand & Chippewa
*Sears, Roebuck and Company
    Kingshighway & Easton

E. St. Louis Bus Terminal
    4th & Washington
Scruggs' Basement Cafeteria
    10th & Olive
Downtown YMCA & YWCA
    Locust between 14th & 16th
Municipal Art Museum
    Forest Park
Fred Harvey Restaurant
    Union Station
Schneithorst's Restaurant
    Lambert Field Airport

Commentary

St. Louis' Silent Racial Revolution
Newspapers Did Not Cover Campaign
To Integrate Lunch Counters
By Richard Dudman

Historians have thus far neglected to give the Midwest, and St. Louis in particular, its rightful credit for its role in an early phase of the civil rights movement. Most histories date the lunch-counter sit-ins from Feb. 1, 1960, when four black college students sat, unserved, at the counter of the Woolworth store in Greensboro, N.C., until the store closed for the day.

The campaign continued, drawing local and national press coverage and spreading quickly to other cities. The sit-ins, which included white students, showed the unstoppable power of nonviolent protest and became the forerunners of the freedom rides, marches and boycotts that led to the end of Jim Crow and the eventual victory of the civil rights movement. Actually, the sit-ins started considerably earlier than 1960. I remember happening upon a sit-in at a downtown St. Louis lunch counter in about 1950, shortly after I joined the *Post-Dispatch* as a reporter. Blacks and whites were occupying all the stools. No one was being served. I asked what was going on and was told it was a demonstration by the Committee of Racial Equality (CORE). As I recall, an editor told me the newspaper knew all about it and there was no need for a story. A recent check of the *Post-Dispatch* files turned up no stories about those lunch counter sit-ins.

Among present-day St. Louisans who took part in those

early sit-ins are Norman Seay and Charles Oldham. Both say the campaign went on for many months in the late 1940s or early 1950s and that they understood at the time that the *Post-Dispatch, Globe-Democrat* and *Star-Times* all had a policy against publishing news of the sit-ins.

Irvin Dagen, now a St. Louis attorney, and his wife, Margaret, were among the founders of CORE in St. Louis. They say they heard about "nonviolent direct action" from Bernice Fisher, a former theology student in Chicago who had become a labor union organizer and was brought to St. Louis by Harold Gibbons of the Teamsters' Union. She told them that such methods had been used successfully in Chicago and Detroit.

The Dagens knew that many blacks avoided going downtown at midday because the only place they could eat lunch were some small restaurants where customers stood at the counter. It was the era of the "vertical Negro," in Harry Golden's phrase. This form of segregation was a matter of custom, not law, but it was nonetheless rigid.

A black woman sometimes would take a sandwich in her purse and eat her lunch in the lavatory in one of the department stores.

According to the Dagens, a mixed group of three or four dozen people, about evenly divided between blacks and whites, planned the campaign to desegregate St. Louis lunch counters. They kept no secrets. They told the police and their friends at the newspapers what they planned to do. And before tackling a business, they always asked to see the manager, tried to negotiate an end to discrimination and, if that failed, disclosed their plan of action.

A downtown Katz Drug Store was their first target. As Margaret Dagen remembers it, no sit-in was necessary there. The management permitted two blacks to come in and be served each day for several weeks to get the counter personnel and other customers used to the idea of an integrated lunch counter, later opening the counter to anyone.

When it was clear that there was going to be no trouble over desegregation at the St. Louis store, the committee met with Katz executives in Kansas City and negotiated integration of Katz lunch counters throughout the region.

In other cases, prolonged sit-ins proved to be the only way to persuade managements to negotiate a settlement. The sit-in at Stix, Baer & Fuller went on for more than a year, says Dagen.

Eventually, all of the major lunch counters were desegregated, including those at Stix, and at Scruggs, Vandervoort & Barney, Famous-Barr, Walgreens and Woolworth's—all without serious incident.

In some cases, she says, a business firm would ask CORE, as part of a negotiated settlement, to join in preventing any publicity. Some businesses that agreed to desegregate their lunch counters early in the campaign expressed fear that news stories about the move would cause a sudden rush of blacks, lined up for blocks to take advantage of the new policy.

Actually, it took the black community some time to get used to open lunch counters, and black customers arrived only gradually, recalls Margaret Dagen. She says, however, that the group always agreed, when asked, to do its best to prevent publicity. But she adds that the newspapers had shown so little interest in the campaign that there never was much chance that a news story would appear.

Two retired *Post-Dispatch* editors who were not then in policy-making positions confirm the paper's policy of not publishing news of the lunch counter sit-ins. The two, Selwyn Pepper and Evarts A. Graham, still generally maintain that the policy was appropriate, considering racial tension at the time, earlier interracial violence in St. Louis and the influence of such racists as Gerald L. K. Smith in the community. They say publicizing the sit-ins might have triggered renewed violence, and they credit the news blackout in part for the fact that lunch-counter integration proceeded peacefully in St. Louis.

In hindsight, Graham says the *Post-Dispatch* perhaps should have published an explanatory article about the movement and its strategy, without naming the particular sites of the sit-ins.

One result of the news blackout is that the history books do not yet mention an innovative, peaceful and successful St. Louis venture in breaking down racial segregation. Another result seems to have been that most of the country had to wait nearly a decade before the lunchrooms began to abandon Jim Crow.

Richard Dudman, Ellsworth, Maine, was a reporter for the Post-Dispatch *for 31 years until he retired in 1981 as chief Washington correspondent.*

For Human Rights
By Irvin Dagen

Ah, love, what to do on Saturday? CORE members are all Saturday's children . . . working all week long for pay . . . but come Saturday they work for love. Like what happened to this one on Saturday, December 17, S-day at Stix.

Billie Ames called him Friday nite, needed a ride to take baby Greg to Mervene Ross' house on Saturday morning, so Mervene's mother could watch Greg while Billie went to Stix to sit. Billie lives in Overland, Mervene in Brentwood and the driver in U. City, so he was up and out in the still dark of the morning, spick and span as all CORE members who go on display each Saturday at Stix. After a wild ride north, south and then down the super-highway the trio noticed it was only 8:32, on the Union Electric clock on Market, so they stopped for breakfast at the De Luxe. They knew that they couldn't get anything to eat downtown and lunch might be hard to get at Stix. So gulp it down at the De Luxe and away again in the car to park on Franklin and Seventh and just make Stix for its opening at 9 a.m.

So begins the long sit. But, this being a special day with tests going on in other stores, too, a couple of the boys go over to Neisner's, sit down, are refused service, still sit. The manager comes over, boiling and bubbling, threatening to throw them out, have them arrested, beaten up; and also to fire all his Negro employees. He'll do this if the boys aren't out in five minutes, but they hold his ear for thirty, and Walter Hayes finally calms him down, and he turns out to be a pretty decent guy. A full-dress conference is arranged for January, after the holiday rush, and the boys and the manager part friends, shaking hands all around.

Then it's back to Stix to sit. But now pictures are needed of the sitting boys and girls at McCrory, Woolworth and Katz Drug Stores (Walgreen serves, so no tests there this Saturday). A camera is loaded with super-fast film, and we have pictures of all the places, with no trouble, except at the Katz store at Eighth and Washington, where the manager becomes threatening, but the picture has already been taken. That's the store where the manager tries to provoke the CORE people by stacking dishes full of garbage on the counter in front of them.

The last photographs are at Woolworth's at Washington and Broadway. Here there is a lily-white counter with plenty of empty seats and at the other end a jim crow stand-up bar in a dark corner. It's so dark it's hard to tell if the pictures will come out, but they ought to be seen by everybody in the community. Perhaps that would at least shame people away from that jim crow place. Can't something be done to make people so ashamed they'll never, never patronize such a place in St. Louis?

Now the boys are back again at Stix to sit out the rest of the long day. The store officials and detectives keep themselves busy buzzing the CORE members, counting them. About half the seats are taken up, CORE members sitting one apart so that the other customers have to sit between them, and they often talk to them, give them the special CORE holiday greeting circular. Many customers leave very friendly toward CORE, expressing sympathy with its aims.

At five the quitting whistle blows for CORE, and some go to a CORE party, others out home, for Billie and Mervene and Greg must get home, and lots of other people have families waiting for them, and that hot meal at home looks good after a whole day of just sitting and no eating. Hot food, hot bath, aching back from those backless stools at Stix, and still the evening to go through. Work, play, read, write, do everything that must still be done. So long a day, but on they go, Saturday's children, and they hope to see you next Saturday!

For Human Rights

Dagen Wants Letters—And He's Willing To Pay
By Irvin Dagen

Have you ever been at sea, at night, and looked up to the stars for guidance? There is the seemingly solid sky (made up of countless particles of dust) and in it, shining brightly, are the stars.

So it is with mankind. One among many will shine. And not only for his own lifetime, but as a guiding light for years after his death. We had one such star in our country for forty years. He shone from his young manhood at the turn of the century until his tragic death in an auto accident in 1938. He was 67 years old when he died, but still shining so brightly it seemed a young man had passed away.

Think of his deeds: Poet, musician, novelist, diplomatic official, lawyer, teacher, organizer for the NAACP. Never a moment slipped by but he was thinking of a way out, doing something about a way out. Who was he? James Weldon Johnson, author of a dozen books, best known of which are "God's Trombones," "Along This Way" and "The Autobiography of an Ex-Colored Man."

If you read nothing else, I think this "Autobiography" will give you an education. When it was first published, in 1912, it did not bear the author's signature. And it was surprising to find how many people claimed to be its author. For at that time "passing" was a more popular pastime.

But there is much more, infinitely more than the problem of "passing" in this book. It is so wise a book that today, forty years after it was written, nobody has shown more understanding or better insight into what the race problem has done to both white America and dark America.

And always the question is with us: HOW CAN WE WIPE OUT JIM-CROW? How can we get over this bump in the road and get on to living as normal, decent, free Americans should be living?

Shall each race crawl into its private shell, admit defeat,

and say that peace will come only by complete, final, permanent segregation?

Shall we state flatly that only total, unequivocal and immediate interracialism will answer our needs?

Shall one race always keep in the background, begging for favors, jumping with joy for even the smallest of these favors?

And is it possible in St. Louis to say: I WILL NEVER KNOWINGLY PATRONIZE A JIM-CROW PLACE? Can we live in St. Louis and really do this? With the schools, the churches, the hotels, the restaurants and the hundred large and small social taboos? I say: IT CAN'T BE DONE! (and that holds for Negro and white).

But I also put this challenge: ARE WE DOING ENOUGH TO BREAK DOWN JIM-CROW? I know there are today enough places in downtown St. Louis serving on an interracial basis, so that there is no good excuse for eating jim-crow. There are printed lists of these places you can get by writing for one to this column.

And there are still other places, not on the list, and which I can't disclose as yet, which WILL serve you if you come in and sit down and ask for service as you ask for it in any other department. And here's another challenge: Next time you are downtown, drop into a restaurant, or a cafeteria, or a department store or a dime store. Go to the eating counter. AND I DON'T MEAN THE JIM-CROW COUNTER. It may surprise you to find how many places WILL serve.

You may be turned down. But you will have shown these people who run the restaurant or the store that THEY LIE WHEN THEY SAY YOU DON'T WANT TO EAT THERE. They say you like jim-crow. I've talked to dozens of them and always they throw this up to me. I DON'T BELIEVE IT. In hundreds of interracial tests we have shown them. But they need thousands of tests, and there are the numbers to make them.

There are, according to some late census figures, about 20 per cent Negroes in the St. Louis population. I believe that's the largest Negro population in any city where Negroes are allowed to vote freely. There's a bill up before the Board of Aldermen, introduced by Alderman Redmond, which would make it illegal to discriminate in eating places. HOW IS THAT 20 PER CENT OF THE VOTE GOING TO MAKE ITSELF HEARD SO THAT THIS BILL IS PASSED?

I want answers, and I'm willing to pay for them. For every letter I get from a reader, with good answers to some of the questions I've raised in this column, I'll send you a free book. Not any book, but one of my favorite books: JAMES WELDON JOHNSON'S "AUTOBIOGRAPHY OF AN EX-COLORED MAN."

In that way I will learn from you, and you will learn from the book. Is that a fair exchange? I think so. So let's hear from you.

Racial Purity Committee
Initiative Petition for City Ordinance
for Separation of the Races

To the Honorable Board of Election Commissioners of The City of St. Louis, Missouri:

We, the undersigned legal and registered voters of The City of St. Louis, Missouri, respectfully petition that under the provisions of Article V of the Charter of The City of St. Louis, Missouri, there be submitted to the legal voters of said City, to be voted upon as provided by said article of said Chartger, the following ordinance, to-wit:

An Ordinance

Regulating separation of the races, and providing a penalty for its violation.

Be it ordained by The City of St. Louis, as follows:

Section One. It shall be unlawful for any person in charge or control of any room, hall, theatre, picture house, auditorium, yard, court, ball park, public park, or other indoor or outdoor place, to which both white persons and negroes are admitted, to cause, permit or allow therein or thereon any theatrical performance, picture exhibition, speech, or educational or entertainment program of any kind whatsoever, unless such room, hall, theatre, picture house, auditorium, yard, court, ball park, or other place, has entrances, exits and seating or standing sections set aside for and assigned to the use of white persons, and other entrances, exits and seating or standing sections set aside for and assigned to the use of negroes, and unless the entrances, exits and seating or standing sections set aside for and assigned to the use of white persons are distinctly separated from those set aside for and assigned to the use of negroes, by well defined physical barriers, and unless the members of each race are effectively restricted and confined to the sections set aside for and assigned to the use of such race.

Section Two. It shall be unlawful for any member of one race to use or occupy any entrance, exit or seating or standing section set aside for and assigned to the use of members of the other race.

Section Three. It shall be unlawful for any person to conduct, participate in or engage in any theatrical performance, picture exhibition, speech, or educational or entertainment program of any kind whatsoever, in any room, hall, theatre, picture house, auditorium, yard, court, ball park, public park, or other indoor or outdoor place, knowing that any provision of the two preceding sections has not been complied with.

Section Four. The Chief of Police and members of the Police Department shall have the right, and it shall be their duty, to disperse any gathering or assemblage in violation of this ordinance, and to arrest any person guilty of violating the same.

Section Five. Any violation of this ordinance shall be punishable by fine of up to five hundred dollars or imprisonment up to ninety days or both.

Section Six. If any provision of this ordinance or the application of any provision to any person or circumstances shall be held invalid, the validity of the remainder of the ordinance and the applicability of such provision to other persons or circumstances shall not be affected thereby.

And we hereby designate by name and residence address the following five persons as the committee of the petitioners, as provided by law, to-wit:

Opal M. Tanner, 3204 Hawthorne Blvd. (8)
John W. Hamilton, 3965 Westminster, (17)
Hermine A. Beck, 3615 Shenandoah Ave. (15)
Don Lohbeck, 1533 S. Grand Ave. (16)
Joseph F. Intagliata, 8116 Vulcan St. (11)

all in the City of St. Louis, Missouri.

And each of the undersigned for himself says: I am a resident and a legal and registered voter of The City of St. Louis, Missouri; I have personally signed this petition and

I have correctly written after my name my residence address in said City.

[space for signatures]

STATE OF MISSOURI
CITY OF ST. LOUIS

The below subscribed Affiant, being duly sworn, on his oath says that each of the above signatures to the foregoing petition was made in Affiant's presence by, as Affiant verily believes, the person whose name it purports to be.

[space for signatures]

BIBLIOGRAPHY

BOOKS

Buckner, John D., Julia Davis, John H. Purnell, and James A. Scott. *Negroes: Their Gift to St. Louis*. St. Louis: Employee Loan Company, 1964.

Farmer, James. *Lay Bare the Heart: An Autobiography of the Civil Rights Movement*. New York: Arbor House, 1985.

Gandhi, Mohandas K. *An Autobiography: The Story of My Experiments with Truth*. Boston: Beacon Press, 1957.

Houser, George. *No One Can Stop the Rain: Glimpses of Africa's Liberation Struggle*. New York: Pilgrim Press, 1989.

Meier, August, and Elliot Rudwick. *CORE: A Study in the Civil Rights Movement, 1942–1968*. New York: Oxford University Press, 1973.

Morrow, Ralph E. *Washington University in St. Louis: A History*. St. Louis: Missouri Historical Society Press, 1996.

Sheean, Vincent. *Mahatma Gandhi: A Great Life in Brief*. New York: Alfred A. Knopf, 1996.

ARTICLES

Adams, Patricia L. "Fighting for Democracy: Civil Rights during World War II." *Missouri Historical Review* 80 (October 1985): 58–75.

Archibald, Robert. "Life in the City, St. Louis: Vibrant Downtown of 50 Years Ago Is Gone; Can Its Enchantments Be Re-created?" *St. Louis Post-Dispatch* (February 16, 1997): 5B.

Dagen, Irvin. "For Human Rights." *St. Louis Argus* (December 30, 1949).

————. "For Human Rights: Dagen Wants Letters and He's Willing to Pay." *St. Louis Argus* [1950s]. Scrapbook. Western Historical Manuscript Collection, University of Missouri–St. Louis.

Darst, Stephen. "Aldermanic Poll Shows Anti-Bias Bill Will Pass." *St. Louis Globe Democrat* (May 19, 1961).

————. "Anti-Bias Bill Is Approved by Aldermen." *St. Louis Globe Democrat* (May 20, 1961).

Dudman, Richard. "Commentary: St. Louis' Silent Racial Revolution, Newspapers Did Not Cover Campaign to Integrate Lunch Counters." *St. Louis Post-Dispatch* (June 11, 1990).

Ladd, Daniel J. "History Lessons." *Universitas, the Magazine of St. Louis University* (spring 1995): 14–17.

Pfeiffenberger, Amy M. "Democracy at Home: The Struggle to Desegregate Washington University in the Post-War Era." *Gateway Heritage* (winter 1989–1990): 14–25.

"Showdown Nears on CORE Job Fight Ultimatum." *St. Louis Argus* (August 30, 1963).

Up to Date with CORE. St. Louis Chapter of CORE, 1951–1955. Missouri Historical Society, Western Historical Manuscript Collection, University of Missouri–St. Louis; also Wisconsin Historical Society.

INTERVIEWS

Written submissions by and tape recordings and transcripts of oral interviews with early members of St. Louis CORE are available at the Western Historical Manuscript Collection, University of Missouri–St. Louis. They include interviews with Joe Ames, Steve Best, Joyce Best, Clothilde Burns, Irv Dagen, Maggie Dagen, Vivian Dreer, Vernell Fuller, Walter Hayes,

Henry Hodge, Mary McClain McAllister, Doris Marglous Nugent, Charles Oldham, Marian Oldham, Alice Parham, Al Park, Ann Park, Rose Parnas, Wanda Penny, Marvin Rich, Vera Rhiney, Bonnie Marglous Rosen, Norman Seay, Eleanor Kendra Smith, Huston Smith, Billie Ames Teneau, Irene Williams, and Norman Winkler.

Index